Quality Management Systems for the Food Industry

Quality Management Systems for the Food Industry is a companion volume to Chapman & Hall's Practical Approaches to Food Control and Food Quality Series

Series editor: Keith G. Anderson

Quality Management Systems for the Food Industry

A guide to ISO 9001/2

Andrew Bolton
Quality Management Consultant
Tunbridge Wells, UK

BLACKIE ACADEMIC & PROFESSIONAL
An Imprint of Chapman & Hall

London · Weinheim · New York · Tokyo · Melbourne · Madras

Published by Blackie Academic and Professional, an imprint of Chapman & Hall, 2–6 Boundary Row, London SE1 8HN, UK

Chapman & Hall, 2–6 Boundary Row, London SE1 8HN, UK

Chapman & Hall GmbH, Pappelallee 3, 69469 Weinheim, Germany

Chapman & Hall USA, 115 Fifth Avenue, New York, NY 10003, USA

Chapman & Hall Japan, ITP-Japan, Kyowa Building, 3F, 2-2-1 Hirakawacho, Chiyoda-ku, Tokyo 102, Japan

DA Book (Aust.) Pty Ltd, 648 Whitehorse Road, Mitcham 3132, Victoria, Australia

Chapman & Hall India, R. Seshadri, 32 Second Main Road, CIT East, Madras 600 035, India

First edition 1997

© 1997 Andrew Bolton

© BSI Quality Assurance Appendices C and D

Typeset in Palatino 10/12 pt by Gray Publishing, Tunbridge Wells

Printed in Great Britain by St Edmundsbury Press Ltd, Bury St Edmunds, Suffolk

ISBN   0 7514 0303 2

A catalogue record for this book is available from the British Library

Library of Congress Catalog Card Number: 96-84773

♾ Printed on acid-free text paper, manufactured in accordance with ANSI/NISO Z39.48-1992 (Permanence of Paper).

Contents

Contents

Preface

In recent years there has been growing pressure for consistent product quality, and a need for companies to demonstrate sound quality management practices in order to meet 'Due Diligence' requirements of both legislation and the quality assurance practices of customers. It has become accepted that operating to the requirements of the international standard for quality management – BS EN ISO 9001 – goes a long way towards meeting these needs.

The objective of this book is to explain the requirements of the standard, to offer advice about achieving those requirements and to indicate what the assessors will look for at assessment time. It is important that certification to the standard is sought to support achievement of company objectives and not the reverse, and of course the standard can apply to organizations and services, just as much as to companies. Thus the word 'company' in the text should be treated accordingly.

Illustrative material has been presented under the logo of a fictitious company 'Quality Food Services' – in this context QFS does not bear any relationship whatsoever to any identically or similarly named business that may exist.

Readers will find it helpful to read the book with a copy of the standard to hand, and are strongly encouraged to read the complete text before taking any steps to prepare for certification to the standard.

Andrew Bolton
Tunbridge Wells
June 1996

Acknowledgements

No book of this nature can be written without adequate experience and knowledge, and quality management in the food industry is both a wide and a deep subject. Inevitably and necessarily one lives and learns from the wisdom and advice of colleagues and friends. I have been privileged to work with many fine colleagues during what has been a happy career, and to all of them, within and without Unilever, I take this opportunity to say thank you.

I am indebted to BSI Quality Assurance for permission to reproduce the Guidelines to the Food and Drink Industry, and to the Hotel and Catering Industry, which can be found in Appendices C and D. Similar acknowledgement is willingly offered to Telarc, New Zealand for the information in Chapter 14 about the Q-Base standard and the text in Appendix E.

To my wife Gillian and our sons Nicholas, Matthew and Jeremy my particularly thanks for the love and encouragement that I enjoy, particulary with regard to the preparation of this book. Gillian has been a diligent proof reader and critic, and the boys have supported my word processing capabilities, or perhaps I should say lack of them!

1

Introduction

1.1 Introduction

The manufacture of food ingredients and products has become an increasingly demanding occupation as consumer expectation and legislative requirements are ever more demanding. In these days of instant communication and rapid transport capability, a problem originating in one country can have serious consequences on the other side of the world very quickly.

Quite rightly, consumers expect consistent quality products that offer good value for money and absolute safety. This is reflected in increasingly onerous legislation which requires careful and detailed management by the food industry. In Europe the Directive on The Official Control of Foodstuffs (EEC, 1989) requires the governments of member states to exert direct supervision on the industry, and in the UK this has been implemented by the Food Safety Act (HMSO, 1990) in which two fundamental changes were introduced into the legislation. The first strengthened the powers of the enforcement officers who now have the duty to approve activities in food premises. Formerly they only had right of entry when they had reason to believe that an offence had been committed. The second change introduced the 'Due Diligence defence' into food legislation for the first time in the UK. These developments focus attention on what constitutes competent quality management in the food industry. Thus it is imperative for anyone operating in the food industry in any capacity to understand the legislative framework.

1.2 The Food Safety Act 1990

The Act defines several offences, namely:

- Section 7, rendering food injurious to health;

- Section 8, selling food that does not comply with food safety requirements;
- Section 14, selling food not of the nature or substance or quality demanded;
- Section 15, falsely describing or presenting food.

Authorized enforcement officers are empowered to issue improvement notices and emergency prohibition notices, courts can issue prohibition orders and emergency prohibition orders, and the Minister can issue emergency control orders and make regulations.

The requirements of the Act are formidable, but it is recognized that it is impossible for manufacturers, traders or retailers to guarantee that every item of food or food product is perfect, and it is inevitable that sometimes a defective product will reach the marketplace. Hence the Due Diligence defence.

Section 40 of the Act also contains enabling legislation by which Codes of Practice can be issued regarding the execution and enforcement of the Act. Important to the food industry are the various Codes of Practice issued in support of the Food Hygiene Regulations. This is an area of legislation that must be observed by everyone involved in the food chain. The Codes of Practice, as at the time of writing, are:

1. Responsibility for enforcement of the Food Safety Act 1990
2. Legal matters
3. General inspection procedures
4. Inspection, detection and seizure of suspect food
5. The use of improvement notices (revised April 1994)
6. Prohibition procedures
7. Sampling for analysis or examination
8. Food standards inspections
9. Food hygiene inspections
10. Enforcement of the temperature control requirements of the Food Hygiene Regulations
11. Enforcement of the Food Premises (Registration) Regulations
12. Division of enforcement responsibilities for the Quick Frozen Foodstuffs Regulations 1990 (revised February 1994)
13. Enforcement of the Food Safety Act 1990 in relation to Crown premises
14. Enforcement of the Food Safety (Live Molluscs and Other Shellfish) Regulations 1992
15. Enforcement of Food Safety (Fishery Products Regulations)
16. Food hazard warning system
17. Enforcement of the Meat Products (Hygiene) Regulations
18. Enforcement of the Dairy Products (Hygiene) Regulations 1995.

1.3 The statutory defences – Due Diligence

Section 21 of the Food Safety Act introduces the **'Due Diligence defence'** whereby

> ... it shall ... be a defence for the person charged to prove that he took all reasonable precautions and exercised all due diligence to avoid the commission of the offence by himself or by a person under his control.

Furthermore for traders charged under Sections 8, 14 or 15, the statutory defence shall be deemed to have been established if they prove either subsection (3):

(a) the commission of the offence was due to an act or default of another person who was not under his control, or to reliance on information supplied by such a person;

(b) that he carried out all such checks of the food in question as were reasonable in all the circumstances, or that it was reasonable in all the circumstances for him to rely on checks carried out by the person who supplied the food to him; and

(c) that he did not know and had no reason to suspect at the time of the commission of the offence that his act or omission would amount to an offence under the relevant provision.

or, as contained in subsection (4):

(a) that the commission of the offence was due to an act or default of another person who was not under his control, or to reliance on the information supplied by such a person;

(b) that the sale or intended sale of which the alleged offence consisted was not a sale under his name or mark; and

(c) that he did not know, and could not reasonably have been expected to know at the time of the commission of the alleged offence that his act or omission would amount to an offence under the relevant provision.

There are several important points to understand:

1. it is up to the accused to prove the Due Diligence defence 'on the balance of probabilities', i.e. more probable than not;
2. the defence has to show ALL reasonable precautions and ALL Due Diligence, not only the convenient bits, and this generally means that positive action should be demonstrated in all respects;
3. the deemed provisions, i.e. subsections 3 and 4, are not available to importers, who should arrange their affairs such that they can use a Due Diligence defence if that becomes necessary.

This then begs the question of what constitutes all Due Diligence, and increasingly it is being recognized that meeting the requirements of the International Standard for Quality Management BS EN ISO 9001 (BSI, 1994) provides recognition of competent and consistent quality management. Implicit in this is sound process control, which can be achieved through application of Hazard Analyses and identification of Critical Control Points – generally known as HACCP (a useful reference work is Mortimore and Wallace, 1994).

These elements, together with compliance with specific legislation go a long way towards a capability to use a Due Diligence defence. Note that this does not necessarily mean being certified to ISO 9001, but if it can be demonstrated that the contents of the standard are being met, then a Due Diligence defence becomes possible. Obviously, companies will only go through the certification process if there is a perceived benefit in their marketplace or in the eyes of their customers.

1.4 What is BS EN ISO 9001?

The ISO 9000 series of standards, together with their derivation from BS 5750, are explained in Chapter 2. BS EN ISO 9001 is the International Standard for Quality Management Systems, which is:

- 'designed to demonstrate a supplier's/manufacturer's/service agent's capability to control the processes (not just factory processes) that determine the acceptance of the product supplied';
- 'aimed at prevention and detection of nonconformity and the implementation of means to prevent its recurrence'.

It is interesting to note that the requirement for BS EN ISO 9001 standards, or similar, is becoming common in other parts of the world, notably in the Middle East, Asia and the Americas. Much of the standard reflects good manufacturing practice and good quality management which should be followed by any food producing or distributing company.

Companies must think internationally, think high standards and think consistent product quality, and should recognize the internal benefits of following this route, namely:

- clarity of purpose;
- good process control, involving identification of Critical Control Points (Mortimore and Wallace, 1994);
- good understanding of the business, not just the section in which an individual works;
- participation of employees, which cultivates motivation;

- efficiency and effectiveness; and
- communication between all parts of the company.

The purpose of this book is to offer practical advice on the implementation of the standard in the food industry: that is to say, the 'how to' as well as the 'what to'. Let it be said, however, that use of BS EN ISO 9001 is by no means restricted to the food industry. It derives from the engineering sector and has been applied to a plethora of industries and services.

This book opens with a discussion about the development of quality management principles leading to the ISO 9001 approach, and then details the necessary preparatory work for the programme. Subsequent chapters concentrate on understanding the requirements of the standard and offer guidance on the implementation. They cover management responsibility, the quality system, relationships with customers and suppliers, internal process controls and audit systems, and the requirements of the training regime. Finally, the mechanism of assessment is described and the book concludes with a discussion of 'What next?', for achievement of the standard is not the finishing line, it is the start of all sorts of exciting possibilities.

While reading the book, the reader should have to hand a copy of BS EN ISO 9001 1994, and is advised to have read the whole book before taking any action.

1.5 Summary

The reader should appreciate that as a consequence of the Directive on the Official Control of Foodstuffs in the EEC, and the Food Safety Act 1990 in Great Britain, it is generally accepted that to achieve a Due Diligence defence and observe good practice, observance of the principles of HACCP (Hazard Analysis of Critical Control Points) and of BS EN ISO 9001, the International Standard for Quality Management Systems, is a necessity for anyone active in the food industry.

2

Quality management principles – why BS EN ISO 9001?

2.1 Quality management principles

In the 'good old days' much of industry operated on the basis that production was the be-all and end-all of the manufacturing function and the objective was to produce the required volume of product at the lowest possible cost. The production team consisted of Producers and Quality Controllers, both reporting to the same manager, and the name of the game was for the Producers to get as much product past the Quality Controllers as possible. Processes consisted of a series of unit operations, at the end of each of which was a 'gate' manned by the Quality Controllers. Producers produced, Quality Controllers tested, and disputes were taken to the Production Manager who tended to err on the side of volume. Piles of 'work in progress' to be reworked were taken for granted and the concept of quality costs was yet to be fully developed. A Chief Chemist's duties were to provide specialist laboratory services and ensure that test methods used by Quality Controllers were appropriate and being used correctly.

In due course factory management structures recognized the need to balance the authority of the Production Management with the introduction of the function of Quality Manager or Quality Assurance Manager, which gave more equanimity to decisions regarding quality issues since agreement had to be achieved. Subsequently the concept of separate Producers and Quality Controllers has been superseded by the modern 'quality assured' approach, whereby everyone is given responsibility for their own actions, operators carry out and record their own on-line quality tests using methods and equipment specified by the quality function, which audits the system and troubleshoots. This demands skilled operators, and detailed training and comprehensive management systems.

In its turn, the quality function can concentrate on strengthening the control systems – particularly developing the HACCP approach – improving the supply chain and auditing the total system. This is the modern quality assurance approach which, in the light of the legislative pressures already discussed, demands complex and detailed management systems and comprehensive record keeping.

How do we judge their competence? Increasingly throughout the world compliance with the international standard BS EN ISO 9001 is deemed to be the acceptable standard for quality management systems.

2.2 What is BS EN ISO 9001?

Formally BS EN ISO 9001 is the International Standard for Quality Management Systems. It can be achieved through qualification in any or all of three ways:

- BS EN ISO 9001 – the model for quality assurance in design, development, production, installation and servicing.
- BS EN ISO 9002 – model for quality assurance in production, installation and servicing.
- BS EN ISO 9003 – model for quality assurance in final inspection and test.

Please note right away that it is a standard for quality management systems and NOT for product quality, although, as we shall see later, it does require clear agreement between customer and supplier about the quality specification of the item involved. The objective is consistent quality at the level specified in the contract; it does not imply that all manufacturers of an item in the marketplace are producing to the same product quality standard. Thus two manufacturers operating at opposite ends of the quality spectrum in the same market can be certified to this standard for quality systems. This is a distinction not well understood by some people, but it is fundamental, and needs stating and restating wherever possible.

The standard is about consistency at the quality level specified by the company.

2.2.1 The development of the standard

The standard started out life as British Standard BS 5750 in 1979. It was updated and republished as BS 5750 and International Standards Organization (ISO) standard 9000 in 1987, and also in that year it was adopted by CEN, the European Committee for Standardization, as EN 29000.

In 1994 it was further updated and re-published in the UK as BS EN ISO 9001 and the structure of the series is now as shown in Table 2.1.

Table 2.1 Structure of the BS EN ISO series

UK Ref.	ISO ref.	Title
BS EN ISO 9000-1	ISO 9000-1 1994	Quality management and quality assurance standards – Part 1: guidelines for selection and use
	ISO 9000-2 1993	Quality management and quality assurance standards – Part 2: generic guidelines for the applications of ISO 9001, ISO 9002 and ISO 9003
	ISO 9000-3 1991	Quality management and quality assurance standards – Part 3: guidelines for the application of ISO 9001 to the development, supply and maintenance of software
BS EN ISO 9001 1994	ISO 9001 1994	Quality systems: model for quality assurance in design, development production, installation and servicing
BS EN ISO 9002 1994	ISO 9002 1994	Quality systems: model for quality assurance in design, development, production, installation and servicing
BS EN ISO 9003	ISO 9003 1994	Quality systems: model for quality assurance in final inspection and test
	ISO 10011-1: 1990	Guidelines for auditing quality systems – Part 1: auditing
	ISO 10011-2: 1991	Guidelines for auditing quality systems – Part 2: qualification criteria for quality systems auditors
	ISO 10011-3: 1991	Guidelines for auditing quality systems – Part 3: management of audit programmes
	ISO 10012-1: 1992	Quality assurance requirements for measuring equipment – Part 1: metrological confirmation system for measuring equipment

2.2.2 Contents of the standard

The contents of the standard are set out in Table 2.2 in the typical format of an ISO document commencing with scope, references and definitions.

The essentials of the standard are contained in the 20 clauses of section 4, all of which must be addressed by the documentation and procedures of a qualifying organization.

Table 2.2 BS EN ISO 9001, Contents

1	Scope
2	Normative reference
3	Definitions
4	Quality system requirements
4.1	Management responsibility
4.2	Quality system
4.3	Contract review
4.4	Design control
4.5	Document and data control
4.6	Purchasing
4.7	Control of customer-supplied product
4.8	Product identification and traceability
4.9	Process control
4.10	Inspection and testing
4.11	Control of inspection, measuring and test equipment
4.12	Inspection and test status
4.13	Control of non-conforming product
4.14	Corrective and preventive action
4.15	Handling, storage, packaging, preservation and delivery
4.16	Control of quality records
4.17	Internal quality audits
4.18	Training
4.19	Servicing
4.20	Statistical techniques

First, **management responsibility** must be described in terms of a quality policy and organizational structure supported by a clear definition of responsibilities in regard to quality, and a summary of the resources available to implement the policy. Most importantly, a member of the executive must be nominated as the Management Representative responsible for management and leadership of the programme.

Clause 4.2 requires that the **quality system** is defined, i.e. all the procedures and methods used to carry out the main activity of the organization need to be specified, together with the standard to which they must be implemented.

Relationships with **customers and suppliers** are dealt with in clauses 4.3 and 4.6, respectively. Both require a clear and agreed specification of the product or item concerned, clear instructions regarding quantities and delivery times, and a performance review between the parties.

Clause 4.4 is important for those organizations wishing to include **design** in the terms of their certification, for the standard requires control of the planning phase, the interfaces between the participating groups, the design inputs and outputs, and demands a design review at appropriate stages of the project to ensure objectives are being met. Finally, the design must be verified and validated to ensure that the customers' needs are achieved.

Good administration of the system is essential if the benefits are to be gained and certification maintained, and the requirements are specified in the section on **document and data approval and issue**. This requires that all documents and databases are individually identified and approved by authorized personnel, are held in specified places appropriate to their use, and that obsolete documents are withdrawn. Changes to documents will also be authorized and the nature of changes indicated in the revised document.

Some companies take in materials or part products from customers and incorporate them into the finished product which is then sold back to the customer. The requirements of clause 4.7 on **control of customer-supplied product** are that records are kept such that use of those materials can be traced and quantities accounted for. This requirement is similar to that of the next clause on **product identification and control** which demands that systems are in place to trace batches of materials from supplier to product, and batches of product from production line to customer on a calendar basis. Documenting the **process controls** as required in clause 4.9 deals with the core activities of any organization, be it factory, office, warehouse, laboratory or surgery. The requirements are that the procedures, working practices and standards of workmanship shall be specified, together with acceptable tolerances, and that appropriate records of these activities be maintained.

Verification and control of these processes involves use of **inspection and testing** methods and equipment, which are covered in clauses 4.10–4.12 of the standard. Basically, inspection and testing must be done using equipment that has been calibrated to the national standard, records of the calibration details must be maintained, and the equipment must have records associated with it, or labels on it, which tell the user when it was last calibrated and when the next calibration is due. Calibration records shall be accepted formally by a responsible person other than the person who has carried out the calibration. Procedures shall be in place to identify clearly, separate and manage any **nonconforming product** arising from the control and test procedures. Obviously it would be futile not to learn from mistakes, and a key aspect of the standard is **corrective and preventive action** – the cult of continuous improvement. Systems must be in place to take corrective action following mishaps, to prevent repetition by designing out difficulties, and by analysing and learning from customer complaints. Evidence must be retained of corrective action, together with confirmation of its effectiveness.

Once produced, products must be **handled, stored, packaged,**

preserved and delivered, and clause 4.15 requires that procedures, standards and records be in place to manage these parameters.

A fundamental and constructive aspect of the standard is the requirement for **internal quality audits**, by which a specially trained group of auditors regularly audits all aspects of the activities, identifying areas where there is discrepancy between procedure and practice, agreeing corrective action with responsible management and checking on the effectiveness of that action.

Clause 4.18 contains the requirements for **training**, whereby every employee shall have a personal training record, and that there shall be a training review, department by department, to establish forward training needs.

Where appropriate, **servicing** needs to be carried out. It requires documented procedures and records. Finally, the need for **statistical techniques** must be determined and documented, together with the methods for carrying them out.

The requirements can be summarized in two instructions:

say what you do, do what you say, and have the records to prove it

and

develop the cult of continuous improvement.

2.3 Results and benefits

So much for the requirements. Many ask, 'Why do it?', 'Is it worth it?', 'It seems to be very bureaucratic.'

The answer to that criticism lies in an appreciation of the philosophy of the approach rather than concentrating on the mechanics. The standard demands that there is clear documentation of the objectives, methods, procedures and standards required in an enterprise, surely something that should exist in any case. In reviewing these matters in preparation for assessment many companies find that the process makes them think clearly about their practices and that they no longer need to do some things they have been doing for years, and on the other hand they find quite considerable gaps in their practices. And once it is done, it is done.

Once this base is in place, then there is a platform for involvement of employees, for motivation, for management of any matter in a similar way, and for management of change. It leads to the cult of continuous improvement, improved performance, less waste, etc. Preparing for certification to ISO 9001 produces these considerable internal benefits: a company can only judge for itself whether there is external benefit in the eyes of the marketplace, the suppliers or the customers, and therefore whether it should go forward to certification.

Small companies often feel overwhelmed by the prospect of preparation for certification – they need not be since their policy and documentation can be very simple and, if products and processes do not change often, maintaining the system will not be onerous.

At the other end of the scale, larger companies find that the system gives them an improved ability to manage the business, since they bring all activities within the ISO 9001 umbrella; and there is universal agreement that the process of preparation brings a better understanding of the business and improved capability to respond to customer needs.

At the individual level, it is often said that the system brings not only a clear understanding of the individual's job but also a better appreciation of its context in the operation, together with a broader understanding of the way in which the company works. And remember that if your company holds ISO 9001 certification or deals with companies that do, there is the confidence that the mechanisms are in place to respond to the customer's needs promptly.

2.4 The administration of BS EN ISO 9001

The responsibility for the contents of ISO 9001 lies with the International Standards Organization, supported by the standards organizations of the member countries. In the UK the responsible body is the British Standards Institution. The responsibility for administration of the standard, and certification of organizations lies with appropriate government departments. In the UK the responsible government department is the United Kingdom Accreditation Service (UKAS), which has accredited numerous organizations to assess companies and organizations wishing to achieve the standard and, where appropriate, certify that the standard has been achieved. Surveillance visits are then made to the companies to verify that certification procedures are being observed and that the standard is maintained. A list of organizations accredited to assess companies for the standard is given in Appendix B, and details of the assessment process are discussed in Chapter 12.

2.5 Summary

This chapter has outlined quality assurance principles, by which responsibility for quality is placed with each jobholder, supported by a technical audit function to verify performance and troubleshoot. The structure and content of the BS EN ISO 9001 standard for quality management systems has been summarized, the benefits outlined and the administration system explained.

3

Preparation for the programme – management commitment

3.1 Strategic objective and scope

In contemplating a project leading to certification to BS EN ISO 9001, it is important that senior executives are clear why they wish to achieve certification, and understand what they are taking on and the resources necessary.

It is crucial that the programme is undertaken to suit the objectives of the company, as distinct from the company altering to comply with the standard. The reasons for undertaking the programme might include any of the following:

- developing the quality management system such that a 'Due Diligence defence' can be used if necessary;
- using it as a basis for managing the business effectively, motivating the workforce and implementing change effectively;
- responding to the demands of the marketplace that competent quality management can be demonstrated through achievement of the standard.

Only when the Chief Executive is clear about the strategic objective can the scope of the project be decided and implementation carried out to achieve and enhance the objective.

There is no obligation for a company to be certified for the whole of its activities. It is possible to define the scope to encompass a specific part of the business, but this does need to be almost a stand-alone area, e.g. manufacture, as distinct from manufacture, sales and distribution. In this circumstance the scope would effectively be from the goods-receiving area to the factory exit gate, and normally execution of purchase and sales orders would be included even if not handled on the same site.

3.2 Is it the right time?

This question cannot be answered until the matters raised later on have been considered, but it is important that there is space in the organization's activities to allow the resources necessary to be devoted to the project. Implementation of capital expenditure, reorganization of production floors, restructuring of the company, introduction of new office procedures, etc. need to be out of the way before starting BS EN ISO 9001, not only to release resources, but also to avoid having to rewrite procedures during the run-up to assessment. For a period of 6–12 months, depending on the size of the business, this project has to be in the forefront of the minds of the executive team and thereafter it has to become a way of life.

3.3 Management commitment and understanding

The first action then is to understand the standard, what is involved and the timescale involved. This can be done in several ways: visit to and discussion with a similar organization to your own, presentation by and discussion with an experienced consultant, attendance at a course or seminar given by the training arm of one of the assessment houses, etc. Every Departmental Head must realize that resources must be provided to review or prepare the necessary documentation and systems in his or her department, and to maintain documentation and practices thereafter.

3.4 Management Representative

The standard requires the appointment of the Management Representative, whose role is to lead and drive the project during the preparation phase, and to manage the programme and activities involved in a successful implementation. This person must have stature in the organization, and enjoy the confidence of the Chief Executive and the respect of the management team. Commonly this will be the Technical Manager or Quality Manager, and referred to henceforth as the Technical Manager.

He or she will usually need to be supported by a good assistant, known hereafter in this text as the Document Controller, who can devote up to 40% of his or her time in the early months to manage document preparation and issue, and a word processor operator who can be devoted to the project for significant periods of time as documentation is generated.

In small companies with a simple management structure, a

member of the management team should take on the role of Management Representative.

3.5 A consultant or not?

Obviously organizations can run the ISO 9001 project by sending the Technical Manager on a training course, and then getting on with it when he or she returns. The likely consequence is a failure to get through document review by the assessors easily, and, similarly, identification of several hold points at assessment which will lengthen the time taken to achieve certification to the standard.

In modern times of very slim management teams it may well be considered that there is inadequate management resource to manage the project up to assessment, and use of a consultant can be considered to:

- either direct the programme, involving up to 30 days' consultancy, depending on the size of the organization,
- or direct and participate in the work, which may double the number of consultancy days.

In either case, a consultant with a track record of achievement of the standard should be chosen, since he or she will not only be able to interpret the standard but also know what the assessors are looking for at document review and the final assessment. However, use of a consultant must not demean the responsibility and activity of the Technical Manager, who, after all, has to manage the programme on a day to day basis. In our case, the use of a consultant with food and drink industry experience is obviously advantageous.

3.6 Appointment of assessors

Many organizations are accredited to carry out assessments to the BS EN ISO 9001 standard (Appendix B), some operating nationally, others internationally. Bearing in mind the lead times involved, it is wise to approach several for quotes some 3–6 months before the project is ready for document review. Prices do vary, and it will be sensible to ask several to quote for the business. Several factors need to be considered before the business is placed. Price is one, but remember that the cheapest will not necessarily be the best decision. Experience of your own sector of the industry will certainly be helpful, and if you are a multi-site organization, a willingness to reserve a specified group of assessors for your business is an advantage, since they only have to be introduced to your organization once.

3.7 Project costs

The extra costs to the company of the project consist of consultancy costs and assessment costs, since the effort of employees involved in the project has been paid for. Between 15 and 30 days' consultancy fees should be provided for, dependent on the brief, and assessment costs will consist of those for document review and the assessment visit. At 1996 UK prices, of the order of £2000 should be budgeted to cover document review and assessment, and £500 should be provided for each subsequent surveillance visit.

3.8 Project plan and timescale

3.8.1 Preparation and communication

The various phases involved in the project are shown in Table 3.1. Clearly the programme starts with the management team under-standing the commitment and deciding to proceed. This should be followed by a presentation to key people identified from each depart-ment who are to contribute to the programme, particularly document review and preparation. The agenda should include reasons for the project, an explanation of ISO 9001 and a review of the timetable. Various videos are available to assist this presentation, notably one from BSI ('BSI Quality Assurance – International Quality Assurance Management System Standard'). Although early activity will be carried out by a relatively small group of people, they will be talking across the site and therefore it is imperative that there is site-wide

Table 3.1 Typical project plan and timescale

Activity	Month
1. Presentation to senior management and decision to proceed	1
2. Presentation to involved management	1
3. Site-wide communication *re* project	1
4. Brief document producers and reviewers	2
5. Draft manuals and procedures	2–8
6. Select and train internal audit team	8–10
7. Site communication *re* internal audit programme	9
8. Internal audit programme	9
9. Training records	9–12
10. Calibration	9–12
11. Establish senior manager's review, supplier review and complaints review	9–12
12. Document review	11
13. Assessment	14
14. Ongoing programme	

communication through normal line management channels to explain what is happening. This also has motivational benefit, since it creates an expectation of involvement and contribution.

3.8.2 Document preparation

So begins a period of detailed activity to prepare the documentation that will become the heart of the ISO 9001 programme – putting in place the '**say what you do**'. Those involved need to be trained in document preparation to formats discussed in Chapter 5. They will collect existing documentation, work with the practitioners to ensure it is up to date, put it into the prescribed format and hand the manuscript to the Document Controller. The manuscripts will then be edited, typed up on the word processor, and issued as first drafts.

3.8.3 Internal audit programme

And so we come to a phase of the programme that is fundamental – not only to success at assessment time but also because it starts to involve everyone in the organization and begins to establish the pattern of life that ISO 9001 requires. The activity involves training the internal audit team, establishing an internal audit programme and preparing the organization to receive the auditors. It is important that everyone understands that internal audit is a joint activity between auditors and auditees to ensure that:

we say what we do, do what we say and have the records to prove it.

It is the key to the organization being ready for assessment and to managing change smoothly in the longer term. The process of internal audit is discussed in Chapter 10.

Once draft procedures have been issued and the internal audit programme started, then there are several other requirements that can be addressed. The first of these is training.

3.8.4 Training

The standard requires that there is a training record for every employee, covering everything from induction to awareness of requirements of the Food Safety Act and ISO 9001 and food hygiene responsibilities to specific job training. Regular reviews are required to identify training needs by department, and individual development needs. Chapter 11 discusses these requirements in greater detail.

3.8.5 Calibration

Fulfilling the requirements for calibration can be demanding, particularly for a large factory, and the programme must be started in good time. In a nutshell, where measurements are being made as distinct from indications being taken, then the instruments used must be calibrated to the appropriate national standard. Detailed records must be retained – the system is explained in Chapter 9.

3.8.6 Management review

As time passes, so the nature of the Senior Manager's review will change from one of project management to review of performance, including supplier performance and complaints. This is discussed in Chapter 4.

3.8.7 Timetable

The timings shown in the table are typical of substantial factories employing 300–500 people with several product types or production lines. Obviously, in smaller organizations preparation of draft documentation will be quicker, but it is dangerous to shorten the internal audit programme, and it must be remembered that 3 months' worth of records are expected by the assessors at assessment time. This implies that 6–9 months is the minimum time necessary to prepare for assessment.

3.8.8 Ongoing programme

Once certification has been achieved then the system can be used and the benefits developed – employee involvement, problem solving, system improvement, etc. – as discussed in Chapter 13.

3.9 Summary

This chapter has emphasized that achievement of the standard should complement the objectives of the company, that necessary expertise should be available, and has defined the necessary work programme. Senior management must recognize that this project must have adequate priority in the company activity, and must not underestimate the work involved for all employees.

Preparation for the programme

DO . . .

- understand the need for a competent quality management system;
- be sure certification to BS EN ISO 9001 complements the company objectives;
- understand the requirements, allocate the right priority and resources, and involve everyone;
- appoint an appropriate Management Representative
- remember that ISO 9001 principles must become a way of life.

DO NOT . . .

- undertake the project because it sounds a good idea;
- underestimate the time and resources involved;
- think that a consultant can do it for you, the company has to do it with his or her guidance;
- think that once achieved, the requirements of the standard can be forgotten, the assessors will return every 6 months.

4

Management responsibility

4.1 Introduction

The standard demands that management is responsible for the quality policy, the organization regarding quality matters, and for regular review of the system, i.e. management review (clause 4.1 of the standard (Table 2.2)). How this can be achieved is the subject of this chapter.

4.2 Quality policy

A good quality policy will define the objectives and responsibilities of the business regarding quality management by:

- saying something about product quality standards and their legality, and commitment to customer needs and expectations;
- giving a commitment to the safety standards of products, processes, operating and distribution procedures and minimizing of risk;
- aspiring for continuous improvement in consistency and economic elimination of defects;
- summarizing any industry standards to which the company is committed, including retention of certification to ISO 9001;
- defining how quality matters are to be managed.

The quality policy is the responsibility of the Chief Executive and should be communicated and published throughout the business in its own right. Naturally it will feature at the front of the company quality manual, which should be made available to all employees. This supporting quality manual will specify where at Board/Senior Management level the Chief Executive has assigned responsibility for product standards, and the definition, development and application of the company quality policy. In other words, it defines the quality management system (QMS) in principle. Note that the standard requires that the company specifies its own quality standards, it does not impose them on the company. The standard is about consistency. The structure and contents of the quality policy and the quality manual are fully discussed in Chapter 5.

4.3 Responsibility and authority

The standard demands that the responsibility, authority and relationships of everybody involved in matters affecting quality shall be clearly defined and documented. This means that in all manuals, procedures, work instructions and other relevant documentation the responsibility for carrying out tests and controls, the recording of results, initiating action in the case of nonconforming product, and defining, implementing and verifying corrective action shall be clearly defined. This implies that the resources for these activities are adequate and clearly identified. Quality records need to identify these activities clearly.

4.4 Management Representative

A member of the management team shall be appointed to have management responsibility for the ISO 9001 project both before and after certification. This person must enjoy the confidence of the Chief Executive and the respect of fellow members of the executive team and the organization in general.

The role involves the establishment and maintenance of the quality system, and during the development of the system the role will be one of project management. Thus it is desirable that the incumbent has a detailed knowledge of the standard, either through close guidance from a consultant, or through attendance at an ISO 9001 lead assessor course, or both.

Once the project is established, the Management Representative is responsible not only for the day to day management and progress of the programme, but also for reporting of progress to the management review meeting.

In large companies this responsibility is generally held by the Technical Manager or the Quality Manager, but in smaller companies where the management structure does not include such appointments, the Chief Executive will appoint the most appropriate person.

4.5 Management review

The standard requires that at specified intervals the responsible managers hold reviews of the quality system to satisfy themselves that the system continues to be suitable and effective, and that performance is satisfactory.

It is sensible that this review is conducted by the senior management team collectively, since this will foster uniform purpose, understanding and motivation across the organization, and demonstrate leadership and commitment to the standard, since the minutes of the review should be publicized in the company. In the programme leading up to certification it will be helpful if this review is held regularly, perhaps monthly, and takes the form of a project review while systems are being developed and established. The meeting will concentrate on progress against the project timescale, quality of work being done, and adequacy of resource – be it people, money or equipment.

As the system matures so the review may take place at least twice a year and the agenda will concentrate more on a review of performance, considering the following items amongst others:

1. Review of quality policy – is it still relevant?
2. External audit reports – review the nonconformances and corrective action.
3. Internal audit programme – review the schedule, major issues raised and action to solve them.
4. Document control – is it satisfactory and up to date?.
5. Quality performance – review of the key indicators and problems this identifies.
6. Supplier review – discuss problem suppliers and action to be taken.
7. Complaint review – discuss the major issues and corrective action.
8. Nonconforming product – discuss analysis of the causes and institute corrective and preventive action.

Matters will be reported by exception and discussion should focus on major items, problem issues, preventive and corrective action, lack of resources, etc. If all is well, move to next item.

These reviews must be minuted and the minutes retained normally for 3 years since they are a prime source of information for the external assessors when they visit for assessment and for the six-monthly surveillance (Chapter 12).

4.6 Complaint management

A responsible attitude to complaints can turn an adverse situation to advantage and improve the image of the business, and that is good reason to deal with them promptly and effectively. The standard does require that an analysis of complaints is considered and necessary preventive action implemented. This analysis is an obvious task for computers, which can be programmed not only to generate the correspondence to the complainant, but also to analyse, categorize and quantify the different types of complaint. The computer programming can be done in house, but it is possible to buy programmes designed for the job. One such example is 'Complaint' (Complaint Management System, Version 2.1, Optima Information Systems, Kings Lynn, Norfolk, UK), which is an advanced software package that offers simple complaint entry, generation and management of correspondence, numerical and cost analyses, and summary of information graphically and in chart form. Complaint data and progress on corrective action should be widely communicated within the company.

4.7 Summary

In this chapter you should have understood:

- the responsibilities of the Chief Executive;
- the need for a quality policy and quality manual;
- the requirement for clear definition of responsibilities and authorities in the QMS;
- the appointment of the Management Representative; and
- the need for, and contents of, the management review.

Management responsibilities

DO . . .

- write a quality policy and a quality manual;
- allocate clear responsibilities;
- appoint a Management Representative;
- involve the executive team in management reviews;
- publish the minutes of the reviews.

DO NOT . . .

- proceed without a well thought out policy and quality management system;
- proceed without clear responsibilities;
- 'not involve' anyone.

5

The quality system and document control

5.1 Introduction

In this chapter consideration will be given to the organization, structure and control of the quality system and its documentation.

It is essential that there is clarity of thought about the structure of documentation from the start, because it can be a complicated exercise to reorganize it once the programme is well under way. There is no universal answer; each organization will find its own solution, but a golden rule is to structure the documentation so that no one section covers more than one topic. If each section is small, individually referenced and numbered, then when any change has to be implemented only a small number of pages have to be re-issued and the task is straightforward. Obviously in small organizations documentation can be concentrated, but in larger organizations it will be more appropriate for each department or section to have its own documentation.

5.1.1 The structure of documentation

Figure 5.1 illustrates the structure of the documentation: the quality policy and quality manual deal with the principles of the system, the departmental manuals specify WHAT has to be done, and the work instructions describe HOW tasks are to be carried out.

Although the principles in the documentation will be the same, the detail of organization in large multi-site companies will be different from that in small companies. Thus in a small company we might find:

- company quality policy, and
- company quality manual and between 15 and 30 procedures;

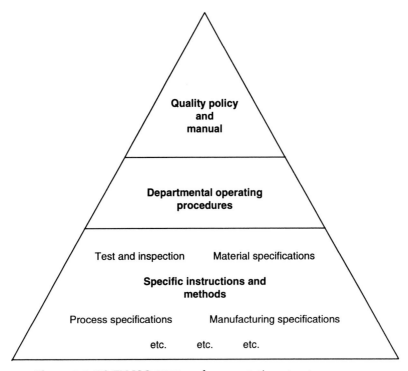

Figure 5.1 BS EN ISO 9001 — documentation structure.

whereas in a large company we could find:

- company quality policy,
- company quality manual and 20–25 company procedures,
- factory manuals and 20–25 factory procedures,
- departmental manuals and departmental procedures,
- work instructions and training manuals.

It will be useful to examine them both as we progress through the requirements.

5.1.2 Stationery

It is sensible to use distinctive stationery specific to the ISO 9001 programme. It should carry the usual company logo and an appropriate heading, done in a colour that identifies it with the 9001 programme. This has two benefits – it gives the documentation a presence and status, carrying a message that the company has serious intent, and it aids document control. Photocopied documents are automatically exposed as unauthorized distribution.

5.1.3 Computerization – the paperless society

The value of generating the documentation on a word processing package hardly needs emphasizing. Modification, re-issue and management are so much easier if documentation is computer based, and in organizations where there is a computer network, then the problem of physically managing distribution of paperwork disappears. The requirements then are that only nominated people can change the text, the Technical Manager holds one hard copy which has been appropriately authorized and anyone who needs to can access the computer programme to read the text.

5.2 The quality policy statement

The quality policy statement sets out the objectives and principles by which the company manages its quality affairs. It may be quite short, as in the example drawn from a manufacturer of own-label products for third parties (Table 5.1, Example 1), or quite explicit (Table 5.1, Example 2) or part of an overall management philosophy as produced by a major branded goods manufacturer (Table 5.2). The important point is that in each case the quality objectives have been set, and if commitment to BS EN ISO 9001 is involved, this is stated clearly. Obviously this statement should be signed by the Chairman or Chief Executive and be authorized the board of the company.

Table 5.1 Quality policy statements

Example 1 Small own-label producer

We shall produce products and provide services at all times which meet or
  exceed the expectations of our customers.
We shall not be content to be of equal quality to our competitors.
Our commitment is to be clearly the best.
Contribution to quality is a responsibility shared by everyone in the company.

Example 2 Major single-product manufacturer

The company produces quality products for export to world markets.
Through a policy of continuous quality improvements we are committed to
  achieving and maintaining the highest standards for product safety and, within
  a cost profile agreed with our customers, world class standards for product
  quality and customer service. In partnership with our suppliers, our customers
  and our employees we are working towards a goal of total consumer
  satisfaction.
As evidence of our commitment we will pursue, obtain and hold certification to
  BS EN ISO 9001.

Table 5.2 Quality policy statement: management policy statement, major branded goods manufacturer

---

Business Aims and Philosophy

OUR GOAL is to be one of the leading branded foods companies in the UK as well as one of the most efficient and quality conscious in Europe. We will concentrate on beverages and foods – specifically safe and wholesome products which can be stored at ambient temperatures. We will achieve our goal by creating and maintaining strong brands which satisfy the demands of consumers.

WE WILL specify product safety and quality that are among the best in each of our market sectors and will maintain such standards consistently. We will do this while striving for operational efficiency.

WE ARE DETERMINED that our trade customers and consumers should prefer and trust us as a supplier because we provide them with the products and services which meet their needs.

WE RECOGNIZE that the success of our business depends on the people who work in it and we intend that there should be opportunities for all to develop their potential, gain new skills and improve existing ones. This will encourage us all to do our jobs more effectively, provide long-term work satisfaction and create opportunities through our business.

WE AIM to foster teamwork and encourage results-oriented attitudes where everyone seeks continuously to improve every aspect of our business.

WE ARE CONCERNED to play our part in protecting the environment and will contribute to ways of improving it.

WE BELIEVE we have a responsibility to the society from which we obtain our livelihood and to the areas in which our Company is located. We support selected activities relevant to our brands and to the Company. We give assistance to selected charities and worthwhile causes as well as to employees who wish to help such activities. We believe links with local educational bodies are mutually beneficial.

WE ARE PROUD of our achievements and our profitability and believe our ultimate responsibility is to continue to run a successful business with above average, sustainable growth.

In support of the Business Aims and Philosophy, the Board have approved the Company Quality Policy which has the objective of:
• defining the key quality attributes and standards that enhance the brands, and the authority for their establishment
• ensuring observation of legal requirements
• ensuring acceptable standards of safety are designed into all activities
• ensuring acceptable standards of safety are achieved
• aiming for continuous improvement in the consistency of quality and the economic elimination of defects.

To this end, the quality system and supporting procedures have been prepared to satisfy the international standards of BS EN ISO 9001, and to encourage a commitment to teamwork, continuous improvement and quality of performance of all employees. The Management Policy Statement and the Company Quality Manual are Mandatory Working Documents which shall be available to all employees.

5.3 The quality manual and procedures

5.3.1 The quality manual

The quality manual quite simply specifies, clause by clause, the policy regarding the topic concerned and where in the company's documentation the detail regarding that topic can be found. The contents list in the manual will therefore be as in the standard set out below, or if it suits to do it a different way, the documentation will certainly cover these headings. However, most companies find it most straightforward to follow the order of the standard:

1. Management responsibility
2. Quality system
3. Contract review
4. Design control
5. Document and data control
6. Purchasing
7. Control of customer-supplied product
8. Product identification and traceability
9. Process control
10. Inspection and testing
11. Control of inspection, measuring and test equipment
12. Inspection and test status
13. Control of nonconforming product
14. Corrective and preventive action
15. Handling, storage, packaging, preservation and delivery
16. Control of quality records
17. Internal quality audits
18. Training
19. Servicing
20. Statistical techniques

For example, the policy for management responsibility might read:

Management responsibility
The Managing Director, supported by the Responsible Manager – the Technical Manager – has overall responsibility, as detailed in Procedure no. 6 – Procedure for Management Responsibility.

or the policy for process controls might read:

Process control
The responsibility for process control rests with the Factory Manager and the Production Manager. The detail is specified in the Production Department manual.

5.3.2 Procedures

Quite often it is sensible for the quality manual to be supported by a set of procedures which are company or factory wide, and apply across all sites and/or all departments. These might be:

- preparation of procedures
- preparation of departmental manuals
- document control
- sales and marketing proposals
- contract packing
- internal auditing
- order entry and processing
- generation, approval and issue of artwork
- planning procedures
- generation and placement of orders
- selection and approval of suppliers
- assessment of supplier performance
- supplier audit procedure
- handling of complaints
- handling of contracts and tenders
- crisis management
- product recall
- allocation of bar codes
- computerized data – access and security
- raw and packaging material specifications
- finished product specifications

NOTE: Not all of these topics will necessarily feature in every company's system, and indeed, strictly speaking, not all are demanded by BS EN ISO 9001. However, many companies choose to manage all activities in the same way and hence these topics are built into their system where appropriate. The important feature is that document structure meets the company's needs.

5.4 The quality plan

The essence of BS EN ISO 9001 is that there is absolute clarity about the whole operation, from taking the customer's order for clearly specified products, to the design and development of those products, their manufacture, and the collation of orders and delivery to the customer. **It is this comprehensive documented plan and its implementation that the assessors will be looking for at assessment time.**
The way in which it is documented and the structure of documentation used are decisions to be taken in each and every

organization that aspires to certification to the standard, but whatever the size and scale of the organization two requirements must be met:

1. there must be a QUALITY POLICY and MANUAL, which define in principle how the 20 clauses of the standard are to be observed, relevant to the defined scope; and
2. there must be an appropriate suite of documents defining WHAT has to be done, HOW and to what standard it is to be done, BY WHOM it is to be done and the RECORDS that are to be kept.

How can this documentation be managed?

5.5 The document system

The extent and structure of the documentation system is personal to the organization concerned, but it may be helpful to look at some examples:

1. A small company employing 50 people;
2. A large, single-product company, employing 300 people on one site;
3. A major, multi-site company with several different product groups, employing in total 2000–3000 people.

Whatever the size and shape of the company or organization, it is important to keep the documentation and its structure as simple as possible.

5.5.1 The small company

The small company will have a simple document structure, probably published in one volume:

Quality policy

Quality manual

Procedures

The portfolio of procedures will cover every activity in the operation and may look like this:

• procedure for preparing procedures
• procedure for document control
• procedure for product specifications
• procedure for order intake

- procedure for material specifications
- procedure for purchasing
- procedures for production
- procedures for quality assurance and laboratory testing
- procedures for packing and order despatch

5.5.2 *The large, single-site, single-product company*

The document structure is as follows:

Quality policy

|

Quality manual and procedures

|

Company handbook

|

Departmental manuals

The list of company procedures is as follows:

- writing procedures
- document control
- writing departmental manuals
- back-up and security of computer-held data and procedures
- establishment and approval of product specifications
- training needs and records
- calibration methods, standards and records
- management review
- internal audit
- nonconforming products
- product identification and traceability
- customer complaints
- generation and approval of artwork
- generation and approval of purchase orders
- approval of suppliers
- review of supplier performance
- acceptance of materials
- generation and authorization of formulations
- pest control
- product recall
- conduct of production trials
- receipt and payment of goods
- stocktaking
- waste management
- weight control reference tests

These are cross-company procedures which everyone needs to be aware of. Every member of the company receives a personal copy of the company handbook. Not only does this contain the terms and conditions of employment but specifically it explains the importance of and commitment to BS EN ISO 9001, the dress standards expected and the hygiene practices required of everybody. There are nine departmental manuals in this plant, not all specifically required by the standard, introduced so that the whole site works to the same system, philosophy and control in which change can be implemented uniformly. They are:

- Engineering Department manual
- Production Department manual – blending
- Production Department manual – filling and packing
- Commercial Department manual
- Warehouse manual
- Information Technology Department manual
- Technical Department manual
- Personnel Department manual
- Occupational Health Department manual

Each of these manuals will describe the activities and tasks going on in the department concerned in sufficient detail for a newcomer to understand what has to be done, by whom, to what standard, and what records have to be kept.

5.5.3 Multi-site, multi-brand companies

Multi-site companies generally have a central Head Office with separate Production sites and Warehousing under separate management. A document structure of the pattern below can be expected. Clearly, at both Company and Factory level it is appropriate to prepare the quality manual and supporting procedures. These will address the 20 clauses of the standard and, of course, additional documentation is necessary in the factories. Many large factories make a variety of products in different parts of the factory, referred to here as Plants, and within each Plant a variety of production lines may exist. Thus it is appropriate to include in the Production manuals the general rules of conduct, in the Plant manuals the general rules specific to the Product Group concerned, and in the Line manuals the operating procedures for the process.

The contents of a Departmental manual in a large factory might be as follows:

(a) General

1. Introduction to Company and Department
2. Company, Site and Department policies
3. Departmental role and responsibilities
4. Department responsibilities
5. Training and records
6. Any other issues

This ground will be covered in each department's manual – Personnel, Engineering, Commercial, Technical including laboratory, Production, etc.

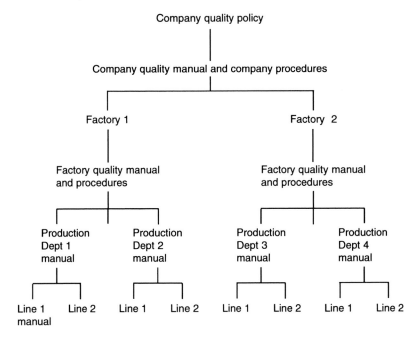

(b) Specific

The Production departmental manual would then discuss the general issues in the Production Department such as:

1. General introduction
2. Dress and hygiene
3. Staffing levels and shift changeover procedures
4. Control procedures: product manufacture, coding, quality and legislative requirements
5. Cleaning methods and schedules

6. Calibration
7. Waste management
8. Training
9. Interdepartmental responsibilities

Following this would be the individual Line manuals for each Line. Topics covered in these might be:

1. Description
2. Staffing
3. Servicing
4. Start-up
5. Operation
6. Process quality control procedures
7. Emergency procedures
8. Order changes
9. Production records
10. Hazards and safety
11. Training

These requirements would be defined in a procedure for preparing departmental manuals.

5.6 Management of documentation

Simple and efficient management of documentation is a prerequisite of a successful system, and is a characteristic to which the assessors pay great attention. Aspects that require attention are:

• format
• content
• authorization and distribution
• revision status and date
• withdrawal procedure

Success is not achieved if adequate resource is not given to the task. Hence the recommendation to appoint a Document Controller.

5.6.1 Format of documents

It is important that documentation relating to the BS EN ISO 9001 system has standing in the company, and thus it is common to find that stationery specific to the project is printed, bearing the company logo and a definitive heading. This is supported by provision of distinctive files to contain the documents.

The stationery will be printed with headers and footers, providing space to contain specific information to aid the management of documents. For example:

QFS Quality Food Services

Document:	**Reference:**
	Issue:
Title:	**Date:**
	Page:

Originated by:	**Authorized by:**
Date:	**Date:**

HEADER

Document name:	Company/Factory quality manual, or Company procedure, or, for example, Marmalade Line manual
Title:	Management review, or Procedure for document review, or Operation of coder
Reference no.:	This must be specific to the document, e.g. CP 018 (i.e. Company procedure no. 18)
Issue no.:	1.2, i.e. Issue no. 1, revision no. 2. (Note: it is usual to move to 'Issue 2' once part of a document has experienced 6–8 revisions, but this is not a requirement)
Page:	2 of 4 – indicates length of document and permits single page revision in a multi-page document

FOOTER

Originated by:	Indicates who wrote the document and who
Approved by:	authorized it and when
Date:	

So much for the design of the stationery to facilitate good management. It is necessary to provide guidance to all authors in the organization so that all documentation has uniform style and content. This is done through two procedures, which assessors will examine early in an assessment. They are:

- procedure for preparing procedures
- procedure for preparing manuals – discussed above.

Procedure for preparing procedures

A good procedure will cover the following ground, indeed may well use these headings:

- Scope: the area covered by the procedure will be specified, e.g. this procedure applies to all documents in the company quality system
- Purpose: to ensure uniform style and content in documentation
- Responsibility: Company Quality Manager
- Procedure: all documentation in the company quality system will be written in this style
- References
- Circulation: all holders of the company quality manual – then specify.

5.6.2 Changes to documents

It is important that when changes to documents are needed, they are implemented quickly, with the awareness of everyone involved, and that the obsolete documents are withdrawn.

The assessors will make a point of checking that documentation in use in departments does indeed match the master copy held by the Technical Manager. So when a change is needed the sequence of events should be:

1. Draft of the new document is sent to the Document Controller (section 5.6.3) by the person holding authority for the document.
2. The new document is prepared by the Document Controller, authorized by the person having authority for the document, and issued to the approved circulation list under a covering note similar to the document revision control sheet shown below.
3. The receiving department puts the new document in the appropriate manual and destroys the old document.

QFS   Quality Food Services

DOCUMENT REVISION CONTROL SHEET

Document:	Company Quality Manual	Issue No:	5
Copy Holder:	Distribution List	Date:	03.01.95

Number	Revision	Date
1.0	First issue	04.01.95
1.1	Section 2 pages 3 and 4	12.05.95
1.2	Sections 4, 6	19.08.95
2.0	Whole document	03.01.96

Authorized by: **Date:**

NOTE:

1. The document revision control sheet is the historical record of the document.
2. The Document Controller must keep a copy of all versions of documents until the next triennial assessment (Chapter 12) in order that the assessors can follow changes to procedures during surveillance visits and at the next triennial assessment.
3. The Document Controller will also maintain a hard copy master copy of the current set of documents.

5.6.3 Resources for documentation

Inevitably this comes down to people and equipment. Since the responsible manager is generally the Technical Manager, it goes without saying that this project will be a major activity in the period up to certification, and a way of life not just for him or her but for everybody thereafter. Since the normal affairs of the company will need to progress also, the Technical Manager needs to be supported by a very competent Document Controller who can manage the development and implementation of the documentation system. It should be recognized that in large organizations the Document Controller may need to spend up to 40% of the time managing the system, and during the development of the documentation there will be periods when full-time word processing resources are needed.

Indeed, with modern office systems it is not unknown for documents to be distributed electronically: this is acceptable to assessors provided it is evident that only authorized individuals can have access to the system to make changes. However, if the system is based on physical distribution of hard copy, then it is essential that all departments nominate specified individuals to be responsible for the department's documentation, to receive it from the Technical Manager's department and to ensure that it is placed in the correct position in the manual.

NOTE: Since a procedure for document control is so essential to the programme, a model can be found at the end of this chapter.

5.7 Computer access and security

The concerns on this topic in connection with BS EN ISO 9001 are no different than those for all computer systems, namely back-up, security of the system against outside influences, and confidentiality. Undoubtedly in substantial company systems these will be the subject of scrutiny at financial audit time, but it is worth summarizing the precautions which the assessors will expect to find in a procedure.

5.7.1 Security

Physically, computer equipment should be kept well away from liquids, which can cause lasting damage to electrical installations.

Whether using server-attached terminals or personal computers (PCs), computer users should have passwords which give them controlled access to computer programs. On server systems this will give a combination of ability to use some programs, and authority to change them. With PCs, of course, it is the only way to protect against unauthorized access.

It is vital therefore that passwords are confidential to the owner, and are never disclosed to others. They should be changed regularly; at least once a month. Computers should never be left running and unattended. If they have to be left they should be left in a secure state.

5.7.2 Viruses

Computer viruses are a common hazard nowadays and strict precautions should be in place to guard against their introduction to a computer system. These should comprise:

- Only information technology (IT) specialists installing software on to company computers, and it must be software that they have approved.
- Only IT specialists transferring software from machine to machine.
- It should be a disciplinary offence for any employee to introduce software, e.g. computer games, to company computers.

5.7.3 Software

Copyright laws must be respected, and only software that has been obtained and used within the terms of the licence should be introduced into company systems.

5.7.4 Back-up arrangements

In substantial company systems arrangements should be in place for daily back-up of the system, with the back-up discs stored off site. Three generations of disc should rotate. Similarly, PC users should back up their files at least monthly, or more frequently if the data are changed regularly.

Remember that assessors have been known to ask for the back-up discs to be produced – and run!

5.8 Summary

In this chapter we have seen the need for:

- distinctive stationery for the ISO 9001 programme;
- tight document control;
- a concise and relevant quality policy;
- a comprehensive quality plan, supported by a documentation structure relevant to company needs;
- documentation that 'Says what we do' in all respects; there must be relevant documentation for all activities.

The quality system and document control

DO . . .

- use distinctive stationery;
- design a document format and documentation structure that meets company needs;
- have a concise quality policy and a comprehensive quality plan;
- appoint a competent Document Controller;
- use a secure word processing/computer system.

DO NOT . . .

- allow sloppy administration;
- permit undocumented activities;
- ignore the need for resource for strong document control.

QFS   Quality Food Services

Document:	Company Procedure	Reference:	CP 001
		Issue:	1.0
Title:	Model Precedure for	Date:	11.05.95
	Document	Page:	1 of 2

Scope: This procedure applies to all documentation within the company quality system.

Purpose: To ensure that all documentation in the system is originated, authorized, issued, revised and withdrawn as necessary in a disciplined way.

Responsibility: This procedure is the responsibility of the Technical Manager.

Procedure:

1. All documentation within the company quality management system will be issued on formal stationery by the Technical Manager.
2. The structure of documentation and authorized signatories is detailed below:

Document	Originated by	Approved by
Co. quality policy and quality manual	Technical Manager	Chief Executive
Co. procedures	Appropriate Manager	Technical Manager
Raw and packaging material specifications	Development Specialist	Co. Development Manager
Finished product specifications	Co. Development Mgr.	Marketing Manager
Departmental manuals and procedures	Appropriate manager	Departmental Manager / Technical Manager

3. Each page of every document will bear a document reference, be numbered, dated and bear an issue status. Each page will be authorized and dated in accordance with the authorities specified in paragraph 2.

Originated by:

Date:

Authorized by:

Date:

QFS Quality Food Services

Document:	Company Procedure	**Reference:**	CP 001
		Issue:	1.0
Title:	Model Procedure for	**Date:**	11.05.95
	Document Control	**Page:**	2 of 2

4. Whenever a new document or a revision to a page, section or document is issued, it will be accompanied by a revision sheet, indicating the nature of the change.
5. Each department will nominate copy holders for its documentation. Copyholders will be responsible for maintaining their manuals in an up-to-date state, removing obsolete documents when instructed.
6. Uncontrolled documentation (i.e. copies that will not be updated) will only be issued off site with the specific permission of the Chief Executive. The Technical Manager will maintain a record of such copies.
7. The Technical Manager will maintain a master copy in hard copy of all documentation issued. This will act as a reference for all documentation on site.
8. The Technical Manager will retain a copy of all documents withdrawn until the next triennial assessment. This will enable the assessors to trace the development of documentation and practices.
9. Under no circumstances will any document be photocopied. If extra copies are required, requests should be made to the Technical Manager.

Originated by: **Authorized by:**

Date: **Date:**

6

Buying and selling – purchasing and contract review

6.1 Introduction

These subjects refer to clauses 4.3 and 4.6 of the standard and are being taken together because the essential disciplines are common. Whether buying materials, etc. or selling the finished product it is necessary to have:

- a specification for the item or product;
- documentary procedures to handle the transaction;
- validation of the quality of the goods;
- procedures governing management of suppliers and sub-contractors and relationships with customers.

Also, taking buying and selling together will remind ourselves that whatever our role in the company, we are all someone's supplier as well as someone's customer. Shades of total quality management – of which more later.

6.2 Purchasing

6.2.1 Policy

The company procedure for purchasing should define a policy that requires purchase of specified items (i.e. a company specification exists) from approved suppliers who can deliver correct quantities of goods to specification in a timely manner.

6.2.2 Placement of orders

The expectation of the assessors will be that all orders are placed with approved suppliers and will either be accompanied by, or refer to, the approved specification for the item. Accordingly therefore, they will wish to see:

- the file of raw and packaging material specifications, and other relevant items, properly drawn up, referenced and authorized in accordance with the procedure for document control;
- evidence that the specifications have been accepted by the supplier;
- the current list of approved suppliers (this should differentiate between active and dormant approved suppliers);
- buyers' purchasing authorities, to verify that orders are being authorized at the appropriate level in the company.

6.2.3 Approval of suppliers

A procedure for the approval of suppliers should exist, setting out the criteria a supplier must achieve to become approved. These may include:

- satisfactory technical inspection, maybe to ISO 9001 standards, and certainly with HACCP expectations, to verify the supplier is capable of meeting the specification; a supplier inspection procedure may well exist;
- satisfactory performance over time, technically, logistically and commercially.

Of course it is open to the company to adopt a 100% inspection approach, and in trading activities where every consignment of goods is purchased against sample this is common. Certificates of analysis or conformity may also be of value.

6.2.4 Supplier rating and performance

Companies may wish to operate a formal rating system for their suppliers, which is reviewed quarterly or half-yearly for example, and the rating then determines the extent to which deliveries are sampled and tested.

Assessors will expect to find clear evidence that deliveries are inspected for satisfactory physical condition and verification of quantity on receipt at the incoming goods warehouse, procedures regarding action if there are problems, and procedures by which goods are released for production, generally by the Quality Assurance Department.

The extent to which sampling and testing is carried out by the QA

Department will depend upon the supplier's rating. For good suppliers it may be decided to test only one in ten deliveries, particularly if a formal vendor assurance programme exists in which formal verification of the supplier's QA and testing capability occurs. In this case assessors will expect evidence of annual visits and inspection of the supplier. Deliveries from moderate suppliers may well be subject to some sampling and testing, dependent upon the nature of past deficiences, and if it is necessary to use unreliable suppliers, then a full test programme on the deliveries will be necessary. This will also apply to new suppliers who are establishing their credibility.

6.3 Contract review

The key elements of relationships with customers are the product specification, handling of orders and deliveries, and management of complaints.

6.3.1 Product specification

The essential requirement is that there is clear agreement with the customer about the product specification, and that due consideration has been given to the order to verify that the supplier has the capability to make the product.

In contrast with the engineering industry, the food industry is not generally in the business of one-offs, with the possible exception of promotional packs, and is selling either branded or own-label products.

The branded goods manufacturer will undoubtedly have a specification to present to his or her customers, who will take it or leave it. The own-label manufacturer, on the other hand, will be given a specification to achieve, and the task is to satisfy the customer that this can be achieved. The enquiry will obviously go through the development procedures (Chapter 7), and the necessary specifications and procedures generated. The quality of the resultant product should then convince the customer to place the contract. Assessors will expect to see written evidence of the commitment of both parties.

6.3.2 Handling of orders

The assessors will look for evidence that consideration is given to each order to ensure that the company has the capability to meet it, both in terms of the specification and production capacity, material stocks, etc. This will generally be found in the planning function of the company, and is especially relevant when the specification is a matter for negotiation, e.g. third-party manufacture. Provision for handling verbal and EDI orders must also be made.

6.3.4 *Handling of complaints*

There are three aspects to this topic – complaints from the customer, i.e. the retailer; complaints from the consumer; and complaints from official authorities, i.e. enforcement departments and legal sources. All need to be dealt with in a professional manner. If handled promptly and sensitively, and the lessons learned and applied, then a seemingly adverse situation can give the company a responsible and caring image with customer, consumer and authorities.

The immediate need is that any complaint is acknowledged promptly, thoroughly investigated and an explanation and appropriate recompense given to the complainant. In regard to retailers, a review of any complaints will be part of the ongoing reviews that Account Managers have with their customers. Consumer complaints, whether received by telephone or in writing, will be dealt with in similar fashion as far as the complainant is concerned.

All complaints, from whatever source, need to be analysed to identify consistent causes of complaint, and action taken to reduce or eliminate them. Assessors will expect to find a procedure detailing how this is done, together with an appropriate summary or report that goes to the Board or Senior Management of the company. It is recognized that there will be a level below which it will not be economic to reduce the complaint rate, but the assessors need evidence that those at the top of the organization have an opportunity to consider the situation.

Similarly, complaints from lawyers and enforcement officers need to be handled at an appropriately senior level in the business, and the procedure for handling complaints should include this.

6.4 Summary

Clear policies should be in place regarding purchasing of materials and selling of products.

Accurate specifications should be agreed with suppliers, and agreement of product specifications with customers is the essence of contract review. Clear evidence that the company has verified its ability to meet an order is required and is particularly relevant to own-label producers.

Supplier management should also involve approval mechanisms and performance reviews. Similarly, companies must take the opportunity to learn from the comments made about their products or services, analyse the complaints made by customers, consumers and enforcement departments, and demonstrate that corrective action has been taken.

Purchasing and contract review

DO . . .

- agree clear specifications with suppliers and customers;
- define buying authorities;
- maintain a list of approved suppliers;
- verify capability to satisfy orders before they are accepted;
- analyse complaints and take corrective action.

DO NOT . . .

- indulge in speculative buying;
- take on orders you cannot fulfil;
- ignore what your customers and consumers tell you.

7

Design and development

7.1 Introduction

Clause 4.4 of the standard requires that there are documented controls to ensure that product design is achieved and verified such that the target specification requirements are met.

If certification to 9001 is sought, then the requirements explained in this chapter must be met, but if certification to 9002 is the intention, then it will be adequate to define where the responsibilities lie with regard to the key documentation required, as illustrated in Table 7.1.

The standard demands that a management control is imposed upon a project plan covering the design and development process.

Table 7.1 Generation, validation and issue of specifications

Standard	Generation	Validation	Issue	Review
Raw material specification	Product development	Co. QA Purchasing	Co. QA	Development
Packaging material specification	Packaging development	Co. QA	Co. QA	Packaging development
Palletization pattern	Packaging development	Co. QA Factory Q & D	Co. QA	Sales
Artwork	Marketing	Co. QA	Marketing	Co. QA
Product formulation	Product development Marketing	Marketing	Product development	Marketing Product development
Product quality attributes	Marketing Co. QA	Co. QA	Product development	Co. QA Marketing
Process specification	Factory Q & D	Co. QA	Co. QA	Factory Q & D

The management control is that there shall be:

design input – design review – design verification – design validation.

If it is accepted that in the food industry the progression of a project might be:

product formulation – packaging development – artwork design – process design and development trials – production commissioning – production,

then preparation of a project plan becomes straightforward.

7.2 Project plan

The first requirement is that there is a clear specification that the design has to achieve, and that a project plan is produced to chart the progression of the project. The key elements of the plan are:

- the sequence of activities necessary to complete the design, clearly identifying the interfaces between different working groups;
- the criterion of success for each step;
- the resources necessary, human and physical, of the necessary calibre;
- allocation of responsibilities for each step;
- any necessary organizational and technical interfaces, including provision for information flow and project review;
- the planned timescale for each step, and hence for the overall programme.

This plan may well be in the form of a network that is available to all participants in the design, and will form the basis of regular project reviews.

7.3 Project management plan

A project plan having been produced, it is straightforward to organize the management process. This will be:

1. approval of the project brief;
2. agreement to the project plan;
3. design input;
4. design review
   (a) formulation
   (b) packaging
   (c) process

(d) artwork
(e) commissioning trials
(f) overall process specification;
5. design verification;
6. design validation;
7. design changes.

A simple development project control sheet, similar to that illustrated, supported by appropriate minutes and working papers, will provide the necessary records to demonstrate that the required management process has been adhered to.

QFS   Quality Food Services

DEVELOPMENT PROJECT CONTROL SHEET

Project reference: **Revision:**

Title: **Date:**

Reason for Issue:

REVIEW   **DATE SIGNED**

Approval of project brief

Approval of project plan

Design review
  Formulation and quality attributes

  Packaging

  Process specification

  Artwork

  Commissioning trials

Design verification

Design validation

Specifications issued

Project complete

7.3.1 Design inputs

The project plan having been drafted, consideration needs to be given to the necessary design inputs to each stage. These might include:

- statutory and regulatory requirements;
- industry standards;
- particular technical information;
- specification output requirements;
- contract review with customer/client, if appropriate.

These need to be thoroughly reviewed to ensure they are adequate quantitatively and qualitatively, and should include the outcome of discussions with suppliers. The finished article constitutes the development brief for the project.

7.3.2 Design output

The standard requires that the design output shall be documented in terms that can be assessed against the requirements of design input, and identify those parameters that are critical to the safety and correct functioning of the product.

In a food manufacturing operation the outputs may well be:

- raw and packaging material specifications;
- product specifications and key quality attributes;
- artwork design;
- process specifications, including process quality control standards.

These will need to be authorized and issued by approved authorities, such as those identified in Table 7.1. At this stage in the development process, specifications may well exist in draft form pending design validation.

7.3.3 Design review

This must be documented and evaluated in terms such that the design output can be judged against the design input and must:

- achieve the acceptance criteria of design input requirements;
- identify design parameters that are crucial to the safe and correct functioning of the product, and which are therefore Critical Control Points in the manufacture of the product.

7.3.4 Design verification

The design must be verified, i.e. as well as checking that design output meets design input, these checks may be supported by activities such as:

- alternative calculations;
- comparison with proven similar designs;
- carrying out suitable tests;
- reviewing design stage documents.

It is essential that there is a formal development review to assess design output and verification, which is attended by representatives of all functions involved and the originator of the project, be it internal or a client or customer. The purpose of this meeting, or series of meetings, is to verify that output has met input at both bench and post-development stages.

7.3.5 Design validation

Finally, design validation should be carried out, preferably on the finished article, by using the product under the prescribed user conditions and needs. These should be a matter of record, and should be carried out using product samples of average production quality. Market research results and complaint data could be included.

7.3.6 Design changes

It is essential that all design changes are documented, approved and reviewed as the project progresses, and are subject to the full management process described above.

7.4 Design documentation

To demonstrate observance of the criteria for design and development, clear documentation is necessary, and assessors will expect to find a suite of documentation, such as:

- project review minutes – reviews of the project plan and progress;
- design reviews – conducted at the end of key stages of the project plan to demonstrate that design output meets design inputs, i.e. design verification; these may well be examined during a project review;

- design validation – to verify that the product does what the user requires;
- design change record;
- design specifications.

7.5 Design specifications

The design having been validated, the detail can be communicated to the company through a series of formal specifications. Companies must specify where the responsibility for generation, validation, issue and review lies, and be able to demonstrate that these requirements have been complied with. Table 7.1 summarizes the suite of specifications that might be typical in a food manufacturing business, and suggests which departments might hold the authority for them.

7.5.1 Raw and packaging material specifications

The essence of these specifications is that they define both the key characteristics of the material and the means of identification, including analytical methods and standards. They should be formally agreed with the supplier(s), and the ability of the supplier to produce to the specification should have been confirmed, if necessary by factory inspection.

They would normally be drawn up by Development and Purchasing and approved by Quality Assurance.

7.5.2 Product specification

This specifies the constituents of the product, with tolerances, after production trials if appropriate, and the packaging format of the unit pack and the bulk pack. It will be agreed by Development and Marketing.

7.5.3 Product quality attributes

It is constructive if Development, Marketing and Quality Assurance agree a product quality attribute statement concerning the product, to facilitate judgement of product samples to a consistent standard. Indeed, preparation and maintenance of standard samples distributed to appropriate departments in the company could be helpful.

7.5.4 Process specification

Following completion of factory trials, a process specification needs to be issued by Development and agreed by Production and QA, which details precisely how the product is to be manufactured and packed.

7.5.5 Palletization pattern

It is important that arrangements are made for the safe transportation of product, and generally this will be in the form of a packaging specification and palletization pattern. Transit tests may also be needed to confirm satisfactory performance.

7.6 Summary

To achieve certification to ISO 9001, it is essential that design and development activity progresses in a structured way and that management involvement has taken place for:

- approval of project brief;
- agreement to project plan;
- design input;
- design review;
- design verification;
- design validation;
- design change.

The output from the development activity shall be a comprehensive set of specifications covering:

- raw and packaging materials;
- product formulation, specification and key quality attributes;
- artwork;
- process specification and controls;
- palletization patterns.

To achieve certification to ISO 9002, the requirement is that the array of authorized specifications is in place.

Design and development

DO . . .

- ensure there is a defined procedure for the management of design and development;
- be sure that design output achieves the requirements of design input, and that design changes are fully documented;
- rigorously ensure that the design is validated, i.e. that it works in widespread conditions of use and abuse;
- require a comprehensive set of specifications to be in place to ensure that correct materials are purchased, and that the required product is manufactured and distributed to customer and consumer.

DO NOT . . .

- carry out development work without a disciplined management plan in place;
- ignore the need for reviews at key points in the time schedule.

8

Process control

8.1 Introduction

This is a topic that is far wider and more demanding than might first appear, and one which involves more than one clause of the standard. The prime requirement of clause 4.9 is to plan the production, installation and servicing and to carry them out under controlled conditions, including adequate procedures to manage the situation when things go wrong, and to provide for adequate distribution of the products.

8.2 Planning

In addressing the subject of process control, the assessors will start by asking the question 'How do you know what you have to make?' and expect to be shown planning procedures which collate orders into production programmes. Typically one might find a long-term projected plan, a medium-term plan and a short-term fixed plan, all updated on a rolling basis at regular intervals. In Chapter 6 the need for absolute clarity between customer and company has been emphasized, and this needs to be supported in the planning phase by confirmation that the company has the capability to fulfil the order.

8.3 Specification and controls

In Chapter 7 the output of the design and development activity was discussed and this included process specifications.

Operationally, specifications and procedures need to be available which:

- specify and pass for use raw and packaging materials;
- define the building standards and any particular environmental controls, e.g. temperature controls, procedures for high-risk areas, etc.;
- specify the process, equipment, staffing levels, process controls and required records (good manufacturing practice requires that the process will have been subject to a HACCP analysis (Hazard Analysis Critical Control Point) to ensure that the key risks have been identified and assessed, and the appropriate controls put in place);
- observe any relevant legislation or codes of practice; this will undoubtedly include actions consequent to hazard, safety and COSHH (Control of Substances Hazardous to Health) assessments under the Health and Safety at Work Act (HMSO, 1974, 1992) and the COSHH Regulations (HMSO, 1988);
- define standards of workmanship or control; these can be written, numerate, standard samples, illustrations, etc.;
- summarize methods and standards of maintenance and service to ensure continued process capability – if external servicing of customer facilities is involved, then a procedure is necessary together with a comprehensive record system;
- define the quality records that are to be kept; these will obviously relate to the results of the HACCP analysis;
- calibrate instrumentation – where measurements are being made, as distinct from indications taken, procedures must be in place to check that the instruments used are within calibration (Chapter 9).

8.4 Dress and hygiene

General standards of dress and hygiene may well have been defined in a site handbook or a general production manual, but if stringent standards are necessary in particular areas, e.g. high-risk areas, fresh meat areas, etc., then these must be specified. Similarly, hygienic practices such as overall changes on entering high-risk areas, the need for alcohol wipes, etc., should be defined.

8.5 Special processes

There are some processes (e.g. baking and coffee roasting) where the result cannot be verified by inspection and testing, and where defects only become evident when the product is in use. The success of these processes is dependent upon consistent application of the specified process by qualified operators, involving close monitoring of process parameters. Pre-qualification of operators, processes and equipment is necessary.

These processes are deemed to be special processes, and the requirements must be documented and records maintained.

8.6 Cleaning

Effective cleaning makes a substantial contribution to sound food preservation, and hence it is necessary to specify cleaning methods, procedures and materials, together with a cleaning schedule, and a system that records when cleaning was done and who did it.

Separate lockable stores are necessary for cleaning materials.

8.7 Nonconforming product

This subject is discussed in clause 4.13 of the standard, which demands that when unsatisfactory product is identified it is managed in such a way that unintended use or installation is prevented. A procedure for management of nonconforming product is necessary, providing for:

- Identification: the nonconforming product must be clearly identified. Use of a fluorescent label, or a uniquely coloured container specific to the nonconforming product is common.
- Documentation – it is convenient to use a form which manages the nonconforming product and satisfies the standard (nonconforming product record, see below). The numbered form provides for date, identification of the stock, quantity, nature of the problem, determination and implementation of corrective action.
- Evaluation – is the stock to be reworked to meet the specification, regraded to a different application, or rejected and scrapped? If reworked to achieve the standard, evidence of the retest results must be retained. These decisions must be made by someone having the appropriate authority.
- Segregation – it is often sensible to move held stock to a separate part of the factory while decisions are made and implemented.
- Disposal – the form must provide for verification that the decision regarding the nonconforming stock has been implemented.

If the contract so requires, use of nonconforming or repaired product must be reported to the customer and a concession note obtained.

QFS Quality Food Services

NONCONFORMING PRODUCT RECORD   No. 0023

Product: **Date:**

Code: **Quantity:**

Fault:

Corrective Action:
  Destroy: Rework: Downgrade:

  Other:

Signed: **Date:**

Corrective Action Implementation

Completed :

Quantity recovered :

Signed: **Date:**

8.8 Work in progress

Where work in progress is put on one side, to await other components for assembly for example, the procedures must be in place to identify, account for and store in such a way that the work in progress is not misused. A specific holding area, either in the production area or in the warehouse is common, and the assessors will verify competent management of work in progress.

8.9 Waste management

In a similar manner to nonconforming product, waste should be managed in a positive fashion, being collected into specifically identifiable containers, and disposed of by documented procedures and records. It may well be that there are Health and Safety, and COSHH, issues that need to be recognized in these procedures.

8.10 Customer-supplied product

If there is a situation in which a half-product is purchased from or supplied by a customer, and then processed into a product which is sold back to the customer, then procedures and records must exist to verify the quality of the half-product on receipt from the customer, account for its processing into the finished product qualitatively and quantitatively, and to verify the quality of the finished product.

8.11 Handling, storage, packaging, preservation and delivery

In the same way that the production process must be documented and controlled, so clause 4.15 requires documented procedures and controls to cover the handling, storage, packaging, preservation and delivery of the product to the customer.

8.11.1 Handling

The finished product specifications should deal with outer and bulk packaging, so procedures need to cover particular methods of handling the product to prevent damage and deterioration, e.g. use of pallets, shrouds, bulk containers, etc.

8.11.2 Storage

Warehouse procedures should define standards of management of the storage areas to prevent damage or deterioration of product. This will cover hygiene and housekeeping, temperature and atmospheric control, management of stock, etc.

Particular attention will be paid by the assessors to the methods of receipt of stock into the warehouse, the holding of stock in the warehouse and despatch of stock/orders from the warehouse. Attention will be given to verifying that stock said by the control system to be in a particular spot or rack in the warehouse is in fact there, and that held stock is clearly identified and can be accounted for. Computerized control systems will be checked by verifying that the rack in the warehouse contains what the computer says it does. Similarly, the assessors will expect to find a system that checks that the assembled order matches the written order and that instructions to the distribution system are clear.

8.11.3 Packaging

In addition to the packaging specifications already mentioned, requirements for marking, including bar coding, must be defined. This also relates to product identification, discussed below.

8.11.4 Preservation

If special conditions need to be maintained, e.g. chilled and frozen products, then these need to be specified and controlled, and records maintained to demonstrate compliance. This applies to the storage and distribution systems.

8.11.5 Delivery

Handling methods and conditions in the distribution chain must be specified, particularly for chilled and frozen products. If an in-house fleet of trucks is used, then procedures for their management and servicing must be in place. If third-party transport is used, then verification that it is fit for the purpose will have to be produced. Similarly, if third-party warehouses and distribution networks are used, the assessors will expect evidence of agreement to procedures, inspection of the facilities and review of performance.

8.12 Product identification and traceability

The standard requires in clause 4.8 that the company has the capability to trace items from receipt of materials to delivery and installation of products. This can also be a legal requirement. In the food industry this is particularly important, since raw and packaging materials are purchased on the world market and a problem with a material in one part of the world can quickly become a product problem in another country. Therefore it is imperative that a supplier or manufacturer can trace his or her product to the marketplace no matter where or what the cause of any problem.

In order to do this, the following are essential.

1. Materials must be received bearing the supplier's batch code, and the manufacturer must satisfy him/herself that the supplier holds production records to support this.
2. Receipt of materials must be a matter of record, as must date of use, since it may be necessary to trace all product containing that batch of material.
3. Use of the material must be traceable to production batches of product, and the finished product should bear a production date code on the packaging. This should distinguish between factories if the product is made in more than one factory, identify the production line if more than one can be involved, and the date of production.
4. Use of any batch of product must be traceable to the orders going out, so that customers who may have received that batch of product can be identified.

NOTE: A batch can be any identifiable quantity convenient to the company – it could be a mixer load, shift output, day's output, or on a time basis, e.g. in a continuous blending operation. The important thing is that it is a definite portion of production, coded specifically, to which specific process records relate, from which the batch of raw materials used can be traced. It is not absolutely necessary to have a high degree of precision about these relationships, since in an emergency the wish will be to ensure that the problem has been bracketed and caught. Thus linkage on a date basis can be adequate, indeed the only way when a production batch might be broken up for despatch to more than one customer, for example. The essential requirement is that in an emergency the capability exists to be able to contact all customers who might have received the faulty product.

None the less, in a crisis management or product recall situation the greater the precision, the better. These issues are fully discussed by Doeg (1995).

8.13 Pest control

Pest control is a subject that cannot be ignored by the management of any food operation, and it is very much a case that prevention is better than cure. Precautionary measures will include: good management of the surroundings to the building – mown grass, hard roads, etc.; insect-proof mesh at open windows; double doors at entrances to production areas; bird proofing of the building.

Pest-control specialists should be employed to monitor pest activity and in this connection the assessors will expect to find a contract with the contractor, a map of the premises showing bait points, visit reports prepared by the contractor defining action carried out and details of action required of the company, the reports signed by an appropriate member of the company, and documentary evidence that the action has been implemented by the company. Pest-control contractors generally supply appropriate documentation.

8.14 Corrective and preventive action

It is worth repeating in this chapter one of the prime requirements of the standard, namely that not only are individual deviations from the norm dealt with, but also that management conducts a periodic review of performance to identify consistent nonconformance, and institutes corrective measures intended to design out the problem and prevent it happening again. The cult of continuous improvement is a fundamental objective and a record of these reviews must be kept to demonstrate this activity.

8.15 Production trials

It is sensible to have a procedure for the management of production trials in order that:

- the trial can be built into the production programme;
- the purpose of the trial is clear, whoever makes the request;
- adequate co-operation and planning occur between departments;
- the resultant product is clearly identified and managed, be it to go to the originating department or sold as stock.

One form can usually be designed to cover these requirements.

8.16 Quality records

Quality records must be structured and completed in such a way that it is clear:

- what the record is;
- what the target and acceptable tolerance is;
- what action is taken when results are outside the tolerance;
- who has made the record;
- that supervisors have reviewed the results.

Process control record sheets need to be structured to meet these requirements and to demonstrate that the process has been under control. However, the danger of records for records' sake needs to be recognized. It is very easy to take lots of data but to have no information – data need to be summarized succinctly to provide meaningful information about the parameter in question.

8.17 Summary

The principles of process control are just as relevant to an office or a service as they are to a manufacturing operation; namely, that there must be clarity as to what has to be done, how it is to be done, to what standard it has to be done, and there should be appropriate records to demonstrate that everything has been achieved.

Thus in a food-manufacturing operation the following will be covered:

- production planning;
- work in progress;
- process specification and controls;
- nonconforming product;
- special processes;
- waste management;
- customer-supplied product;
- pest control;
- dress and hygiene;
- product identification and traceability;
- cleaning schedules and procedures;
- handling, storage, packing and delivery;
- corrective and preventive action;
- quality records.

Process control

DO . . .

- ensure that process specifications are comprehensive, with standards and tolerances;
- base controls on HACCP analysis;
- ensure that standards of dress and hygiene are appropriate;
- ensure that process control records are comprehensive, and are reviewed by responsible management at the end of a shift;
- ensure that procedures are in place for managing cleaning, non-conforming product, waste and pest control;
- ensure that identification and traceability are possible from material supplier to consumer.

DO NOT . . .

- take risks;
- allow sloppy record keeping;
- fail to react to out-of-specification or nonconforming situations.

9

Inspection, measuring and testing – calibration

9.1 Introduction

Inspection, measuring and testing is a theme that runs right through a manufacturing operation from receipt of materials, to process control and approval of finished goods, and includes management of the equipment used in the tests, and the measured product. Equipment used to take measurements, as distinct from giving an indication, must be properly calibrated to the appropriate national standard. Note the distinction between measurement and indication. If the response to a reading is one of precision, then it is a measurement, but if a wide tolerance is involved or the reading is taken for awareness only, then it is an indication and calibration is not necessary.

The following clauses of the standard are relevant:

4.10 Inspection and testing
4.11 Control of inspection, measuring and test equipment
4.12 Inspection and test status

9.2 Inspection and testing

The general principle is that the quality plan will specify all requirements for inspection and testing, including the tests to be used, the acceptable tolerances, and the form of record to be kept. Additionally, instructions will be given regarding action to be taken in the event of the test being failed, and management of the affected goods. Note that this includes any tasting activities, where it is necessary to show that the tasters are capable of making the required judgement (section 9.3).

9.2.1 Incoming materials

The standard requires that incoming materials have been verified as fit for purpose. This topic has been dealt with fully in Chapter 6, in which the intricacies of supplier management have been explained. The fundamental point is that in order to make use of the Due Diligence defence a company must be able to show positive action to assure the quality of incoming materials.

9.2.2 Process control

The documentation relative to the production operation must specify the control tests necessary, the acceptable tolerances and particularly action to be taken regarding failed goods – this includes their physical management and the decision-making process regarding their management. Reject goods must be clearly identified, either by an appropriate label or by retention in a colour-coded container, for example, and decisions concerning rectification or disposal must be made by the defined authority and be a matter of record (Chapter 8).

Records of process control measurements must be kept, recording the identity of any calibrated equipment used, the identity of the operator and the measurement results, and action taken regarding failed product.

9.2.3 Final inspection and testing

The manufacturer must be able to demonstrate that the product meets the customer's requirement or the specification for the product, either through end-of-line tests, or, if a quality assurance approach has been taken, by reviewing the process records and releasing the products.

9.2.4 Inspection and test records

Details must be kept of all test records, and should identify who carried out the tests, the results and the identity of the authority who released the product. All appropriate records need to be inspected, signed by the approving authority and retained for prescribed periods.

9.3 Control of inspection, measuring and test equipment – calibration

9.3.1 Principles of measurement

The requirement is that all equipment that is used to take measurements is properly calibrated, and that the calibration details are a matter of record. Obviously this is to provide a sound technical basis to all control mechanisms.

NOTE: The requirement applies to measuring equipment as distinct from equipment used to give an indication. As mentioned above, if the reading is being taken merely to indicate adherence to broad limits and there is minimal reaction to the reading, then calibration of the instrument is not required. On the contrary, if measurement is required to tight tolerances and control action is a consequence, then the instrument must be calibrated.

The decision regarding measurement or indication lies with the company being assessed, but clearly the assessors will challenge the decision if they think an instrument that is not calibrated should be.

The criteria of a sound calibration system are:

- a calibration policy;
- a schedule of instruments to be calibrated;
- a procedure for calibration which includes the required tolerances;
- records of the calibration details.

9.3.2 Calibration policy

The calibration policy for the company/site should be stated in the quality manual and may well read as follows:

All critical inspection, measuring and test equipment will be calibrated at specified intervals using specified methodology. Calibrated instruments will be so identified and a detailed record of the calibration maintained for each instrument.

An inventory of inspection, measuring and test equipment to be calibrated, together with the method of calibration, is maintained in the appropriate departmental manual. This includes the target reading and acceptable tolerances and the standard against which the calibration is to be made.

When an instrument fails its calibration test, the implication for all product made since the last acceptable calibration will be reviewed by the Quality Manager and the Manufacturing Manager. In order to minimize the implications of this requirement, it is common in many factories to superimpose an internal weekly or monthly calibration check, particularly for weight management, volumes and number controls. A formally certified set of master weights is used to prepare a set of test weights – salt packs for example – to check that weighing equipment is still within specified tolerance. If the test is failed, only a week's production is at risk.

Overall responsibility for the calibration programme rests with the Quality Manager (or whoever is nominated).

9.3.3 Calibration schedule

This will be maintained by the responsible department, generally the Engineering and/or Quality Department. It will consist of a list of instruments, probably identified by name, asset number and location, the reference number of the calibration procedure to be used, and the calibration frequency.

These schedules and procedures may exist in hard copy supported by a diary-based bring-up system to identify which instruments have to be calibrated, when; or in large, complicated sites they could well be on a computerized maintenance management system. For the benefit of users, all calibrated instruments should bear a label recording the last calibration date and the due date of the next calibration.

9.3.4 Calibration procedure and records

Several requirements have to be met:

1. The calibration procedure shall be on record, either specified by the company or provided by a specialist contractor to the company's satisfaction.
2. The acceptable targets and tolerances must be stated.
3. The status of the calibrating equipment must be recorded, such that it can be traced back to a national standard.
4. All calibration data must be recorded and signed by the person carrying out the work, and signed for by the company employee who accepts the calibration.
5. Calibrated equipment should be labelled with the date of the calibration and the projected date of the next calibration.

Calibration is discussed further in Wilson and Weir (1995).

9.4 Inspection and test status

The QMS must define how the status of product is to be defined in the production process. In continuous processes it is common to declare that all product is sound unless it is held and labelled accordingly. In non-continuous processes it is usual to label batches of product with their status.

Unsatisfactory product must be clearly identified as such and separated from satisfactory product while decisions are taken regarding corrective action. The decision and its implementation must be a matter of record (Chapter 8).

9.5 Summary

1. Inspection and testing. The targets, tolerances and methodology for all tests, be they incoming goods, process control or finished product testing, must be specified.
2. Calibration. For all instrumentation used for measurement, as opposed to merely giving an indication, there must be:
   - a calibration schedule;
   - calibration methodology traceable to national standards, specifying required targets and tolerances;
   - a record of calibration details;
   - evidence of review and acceptance of the calibration by someone other than the person who performed the calibration.
3. Inspection and test status. There must be absolute clarity regarding the test status of materials, work in progress and finished product, particularly for any nonconforming items.

Inspection, measuring and testing – calibration

DO . . .

- be clear about measurement as opposed to indication;
- specify method, target and tolerance for all measurements;
- produce an inventory of all instruments used for measurement, together with their calibration schedule;
- ensure clarity *re* calibration methods, standards, targets and tolerances;
- ensure calibration details are recorded and retained, and that calibrations are reviewed and accepted by responsible management – this must be someone separate from the person who carried out the calibration;
- be sure that the status of all materials, work in progress and finished products is clear; this particularly applies to nonconforming items.

DO NOT . . .

- forget to specify the tolerances needed for each measurement and each calibration;
- forget that the calibration certificate should be signed by a responsible member of management who has not performed the calibration, to indicate review and acceptance of the calibration;
- underestimate the care and attention that calibration management requires.

QFS   Quality Food Services

Document:	Company Procedure	**Reference:** **Issue:**	CP 024 1.0
Title:	Laboratory Procedures – Calibration of Equipment	**Date:** **Page:**	13-6-95 2 of 2

Test Equipment Calibration Schedule

Equipment	Location	Calibration		Responsibility	Checked
		Method	Period		by
Weigh Scales	Production	6.2	monthly	PQC	QA
		Ext. Contract	annually	Ext. contract	QA
Calibration Weights	Production	6.4	3-monthly	QA	QA
	Technical Dept.	6.4	3-yearly	Ext. contract	Tech. Mgr

Originated by: **Authorized by:**

Date: **Date:**

10

Internal quality audit

10.1 Introduction

The standard requires in clause 4.17 that the quality system is audited thoroughly by an appropriately trained team to ensure that the requirements of the standard are being met, and that documented procedures are being observed – in short, that we are

doing what we say, and have the records to prove it.

But the activity of the internal quality audit (IQA) team is more than merely a review of practice; it is a vehicle for facilitating constructive improvement – the cult of continuous improvement – and for this to happen there needs to be a set of audit procedures, a trained team of auditors working to a schedule, and an understanding in the company that the internal audit programme is participative, is there to ensure that the company is working smoothly, and that when the assessors arrive for intermediate inspections (typically every 6 months) everything will be in order, and thus there can be pride in achieving and maintaining certification to the standard.

10.2 Internal audit procedure

The assessors will expect to find a procedure that defines how internal audits are to be conducted, reported on, reviewed and followed up. It should be supported by a list of approved internal auditors (see below) and a forward timetable for internal audits. A model procedure can be found at the end of the chapter.

The audit programme will be managed by the Technical Manager, who should plan to audit each department against all clauses of the standard at least annually. In practice this probably means two or three audits during a 12-month period.

Auditors should be trained to approach the audit in a structured way by:

- deciding the scope of the audit, i.e. the topics/clauses of the standard to be covered – the Technical Manager may influence this since he or she has to ensure that the standard is fully covered during the year, but auditors must be allowed to decide the scope, dependent on previous reports, leads from audits of other departments etc.;
- preparing a checklist of questions – audits will progress smoothly and efficiently if the line of questioning is prepared; in any audit the auditors should always check that the documentation in the department concerned is up to date, and matches the issue status in the master copy;
- conducting the audit and preparing a summary of nonconformances found;
- participating in a review meeting with the management of the department concerned;
- carrying out any follow-up audits, as required by the Technical Manager.

10.3 The audit schedule

The requirement is that audits should be scheduled on the basis of the status and importance of the activity concerned. Common sense suggests this should be at least annually, but bearing in mind that control is necessary, action from review meetings needs to be followed up and progress needs to be demonstrated, an audit at least every 6 months is sensible. This helps to achieve the requirement that all clauses of the standard are looked at in every department. Since the assessors may be conducting a surveillance visit every 6 months, such a frequency will demonstrate control and progress to them.

In meeting the requirement that all clauses of the standard are examined in all departments, the Technical Manager may choose to have an audit of a clause of the standard carried out across the company, as distinct from looking at all activities in a department. Training, quality records, and calibration lend themselves to this treatment. Any new procedures and activities should be audited soon after their introduction into the company.

The schedule should specify the date of the audit, i.e. week commencing, the department or topic concerned, and the auditors concerned. It should be circulated widely so that the timing of audits is known in advance, and particularly so that management know when auditors will be away from their own jobs.

10.4 Selection and training of auditors

10.4.1 Selection

This needs to be done with extreme care, since a successful internal audit programme is crucial to the implementation of the standard and a constructive quality management system. Clearly, the number of auditors depends upon the size of the business and the audit schedule, but a rule of thumb is that an auditor should carry out an audit at least once a quarter.

Some companies draw their auditors totally from the Quality Assurance function, and indeed there is nothing wrong with that, but in large companies this may not be practical. Certainly it is more constructive to draw auditors from the breadth of the organization and from a diagonal slice through its structure. The audit team must be a blend of assistant managers, technical specialists, office and factory employees – all of whom must meet two criteria:

- they must have the personality and intelligence to talk to anyone in the company;
- they must be accepted by their peers.

10.4.2 Training

The training of the internal audit team must be thorough and supervised by someone with substantial experience of BS EN ISO 9001. The programme should have the objectives of:

- reviewing quality management principles;
- imparting an understanding of the requirements of the standard;
- teaching how to carry out an audit;
- supervised practice;
- judgement of competence, leading to the status of approved auditor.

The training programme will therefore consist of:

- internal audit training;
- practical audit with supervision;
- review session.

The content of this programme is discussed fully in section 10.6, but it is appropriate to discuss now the contribution and preparation of the auditees to the internal audit.

10.5 Preparation of the auditees

It is important to recognize that apart from an awareness that the company is undertaking the project and that documentation is being drafted, the majority of the company will not yet have been involved in the project, and therefore they need a progress report and to be prepared to participate in the internal audit process. The Technical Manager should therefore issue a briefing sheet, probably through the management review meeting, to be communicated to everyone via normal line management communication channels. The briefing should:

- summarize progress to date;
- point out that the objective of the internal audit programme is for everyone to work together to ensure that:

we say what we do, do what we say, and have the records to prove it

and thus have everything in order for the assessors;
- summarize the forward audit schedule.

10.6 The internal audit training programme

A typical agenda for audit training day is summarized in Table 10.1. The programme will be conducted by the Technical Manager, supported by a consultant or colleague with the necessary experience. Obviously the introduction will deal with logistic and domestic matters, and then summarize the content of the programme. It can, of course, be done in two half days, but these should not be far apart.

Table 10.1 Agenda for internal audit training programme

Introduction

1. Quality and quality assurance
2. BS EN ISO series. Why? What is it?
3. The documentation system
4. System for quality management audits
5. Audit preparation

LUNCH

6. Syndicates – audit checklist
7. Performing the audit
8. Personal skills
9. Syndicates – preparing the nonconformance report
10. Reports, records and follow-up
11. Internal audit programme
12. Review

10.6.1 *Quality and quality assurance*

Bearing in mind that the auditors will be from a cross-section of the factory community, it is sensible to start by reviewing some principles of quality management. The objectives of the company will undoubtedly include those of consistent quality standards, expressed in the company quality policy, with a commitment to certification to the standard.

Quality may be defined as:

- conformance with (the customer's) requirements;
- fitness for purpose.

It is not achieved through control by inspectors or auditors, but by the people who do the work, using processes, procedures and equipment that have been designed to achieve the required result. That is to say that quality has been assured through all the planned and systematic actions necessary to provide adequate **confidence** that a structure, system, component or product will perform satisfactorily in service or use.

It is the element of **consistency** that the standard aims to facilitate.

10.6.2 *BS EN ISO 9001 Why? What is it?*

There are both quality management and legislative reasons for aspiring to certification to BS EN ISO 9001. The objective of consistent quality has already been discussed above, but it is useful to understand the legislative reasons for holding certification. These have been explained in Chapter 2, but they are worth repeating.

The EEC Directive on The Official Control of Foodstuffs (EEC, 1989) requires Member States to supervise the food industry directly within its remit. In the UK this responsibility was implemented in The Food Safety Act of 1990, which also introduced to food legislation the Due Diligence defence, which requires that you prove that you have 'taken all reasonable precautions and exercised all due diligence to avoid the commission of the offence by yourself or by a person under your control'. This then begs the question of what constitutes competent standards and Due Diligence.

It has become recognized increasingly that observance of BS EN ISO 9001 and HACCP (Hazard Analysis Critical Control Point) go a long way to satisfying the requirements, hence the wide move to achieving the detail of the standard, if not necessarily achieving certification. Note that Due Diligence implies ALL reasonable precautions and diligence, not merely those that are convenient.

The Technical Manager and/or consultant should then work

through every clause of the standard, explaining the meaning and requirements, maybe using the BSI Video ('BSI Quality Assurance – International Quality Assurance Management System Standard') or something similar. Each member of the audit team should have their own copy of the standard, together with explanatory notes.

10.6.3 Company documentation

It is imperative that the structure and content of the documentation is understood by the team; indeed, they need to be familiar with it. Copies should be available and they should be conducted through the hierarchy from quality policy, quality manual and procedures, to manuals and work instructions (Chapter 5).

10.6.4 System for quality management audits

It has been shown that the standard demands:

- comprehensive specifications, with formal control of paperwork, discipline regarding change, and written work instructions where appropriate;
- detailed records; necessary to provide evidence of conformance of product and system to the customer's requirements, and that the QA system complies with the standard.

In other words, the quality system is based on **formality**, which itself permits **objectivity**. The audit is seeking to verify that the company

says what it does, does what it says, and has the records to prove it.

Remember if there is no record, it hasn't been done.

A quality management audit is a systematic investigation of the intent, implementation and the effectiveness of selected aspects of the quality systems of an organization or department.

It is a formal activity carried out against *aides-mémoire*, procedures, checklists, policy, etc., to examine objective evidence independently and verify, or otherwise, compliance with specified requirements.

The auditor is setting out to:

- verify that intent is summarized in the documentation;
- establish the extent to which intent has been implemented;
- establish whether the practice is effective in achieving the objective of the procedure;
- verify that appropriately trained staff are carrying out the tasks observed;
- examine interfaces between colleagues, departments, companies, etc.

The auditor is looking for objective evidence, i.e. evidence which exists, is uninfluenced by emotion or prejudice, can be stated, documented and verified. It can be qualitative or quantitative.

An audit can be:

- first party, i.e. internal audit;
- second party, i.e. one company on another, not necessarily by visit, it can be an examination of track record;
- third party, by external assessor.

But whatever type of audit, it will progress through the four phases of

planning – execution – review – close-out.

Examples of documentation referred to can be found in the model procedure at the end of the chapter.

10.6.5 Audit preparation

The immediate decision facing an auditor is the **scope** of the intended audit. This may be influenced partly by the needs of the Technical Manager, but should also emerge from the auditor's assessment of available information. This will include:

- available documentation;
- management priorities;
- quality problems, customer complaints;
- previous audit results;
- product information;
- auditor experience;
- outcome of preliminary visit.

This will enable the auditor to prepare a **checklist**. Why? Well there is little point in entering a department with a blank sheet of paper, following your nose and wondering what to do next. That does not work. Preparing a checklist offers considerable benefits:

- it aids formality;
- it maintains objectivity;
- it requires research;
- it maintains pace and timing;
- it provides historical reference;
- it reduces pressure during the audit.

The first item on the checklist should always be documentation, to verify that documentation in the department being audited matches the master copy and that document control procedures are being observed. But remember to study the relevant documents – they tell the way things are, advise employees, impress visitors – and aid auditors! The checklist should remind the auditor what to look at, what to look for, and to enquire what happens when systems fail. But the checklist is the servant not the master – if the audit trail takes you beyond the checklist, fine.

In pursuing a line of audit there is no finer prompt than Kipling's poem:

> I keep six honest serving men
> They taught me all they knew,
> Their names are WHAT and WHY and WHEN
> and HOW and WHERE and WHO.

10.6.6 Case study 1 – audit checklist

At this stage in the training day the auditors should be split into syndicates of three or four and given the task of preparing a checklist. For this purpose the Technical Manager should select a topic and define the scope from the company documentation and ask the syndicates to prepare the checklist. Select different topics for each pair of syndicates, allow 40–45 minutes for preparation and then ask a syndicate to present its findings. The other syndicate of the pair can then comment.

10.6.7 Performing the audit

The audit will progress through the phases of being arranged, conducting the opening meeting, carrying out the audit and holding the closing meeting.

1. Arranging the meeting – although the audit schedule will have been programmed for a specific week, the auditor should make the detailed arrangements for the audit him or herself with the management of the department concerned. This helps the formality, creates contact, and offers the auditor the opportunity to request a brief tour of the department if it is one with which the auditor is unfamiliar.
2. Opening the meeting – the auditor will introduce him or herself, identify the scope of the audit, agree the programme, and summarize the reporting method. The department should provide a senior member to act as guide, ensure that the auditor receives full answers, and indeed asks the question of the right person in the department.

3. Carrying out the audit – the auditor should move purposefully through the checklist, covering the points and moving on if all is well. On the other hand, discrepancies, facts and observations should be pursued until it becomes clear whether or not a discrepancy exists and a nonconformance is recorded. A nonconformance is a variation from a specified situation, or a violation of the standard. It might be failure to meet a condition of the contract, a product standard, variation of procedure or work instruction, etc. Nonconformances should be agreed clearly with the guide at the time they become evident, and a view developed regarding the seriousness of the problem.
4. Closing meeting – when the audit is complete the auditor should complete the nonconformance report, review the results with the management of the department and leave a copy.

10.6.8 Personal skills

The auditor must recognize and understand that the role is not that of policeman nor of a consultant, but one of facilitator, acting as a catalyst for improvement, an interface between supplier, customer and colleague. And everyone must recognize that they in turn are someone's supplier and someone's customer.

The auditor is a diplomat, needing to be flexible, tactful but at the same time firm and persistent, at all times acting with integrity and demonstrating excellent communication skills.

10.6.9 Case study 2 – preparing a report

The course works in syndicates once again. The Technical Manager will have prepared scenarios reflecting 'What the auditor saw and heard'. The texts will describe some observations that are clearly satisfactory, some that are clearly nonconformances, and particularly some that are in the grey area, where perhaps further questions have to be asked, or judgement is necessary.

The task of the syndicates is to prepare the nonconformances and decide which clauses of the standard have been contravened.

10.6.10 Reports, records and follow-up

As the audit proceeds there will arise a situation where the facts indicate that there is a failure in part or all of the system. Such an event is a nonconformance. Numerous nonconformances can be found in an audit, but it is unlikely that they will have equal importance or significance. Conversely, no nonconformances might have been found, even though they actually exist. Two principles apply:

- it is not a witch hunt; if you get satisfactory answers to your questions, there is no need to pursue the matter;
- there must be hard evidence to sustain a nonconformance.

Once facts are established they must be agreed with the auditee and written up in a way that facilitates corrective action, using local terminology where appropriate. A nonconformance report should be brief and cover:

- exact observation of the facts;
- where it was found;
- what was found;
- why it was a discrepancy;
- who was there.

The nonconformances will vary in importance, so it is helpful to classify them as major or minor by asking two questions:

- what could go wrong if the deficiency is not corrected?
- what is the likelihood of it going wrong?

The completed nonconformance report (example at end of chapter) should be returned together with the checksheet, to the Technical Manager. The Technical Manager will then convene a review meeting with the management of the department concerned, attended by the auditor, to agree corrective action and the timescale for completion. These decisions should be recorded on the review summary sheet (end of chapter) and the Technical Manager will file this together with the checklist and nonconformance report. In due course he will arrange for a follow-up audit to verify that corrective action has been carried out and has been effective.

In large sites, keeping track of the need for follow-up audits and closing out corrective action can be a problem for the Technical Manager, who will need to demonstrate to the assessors that an effective follow-up system exists. A diary-based 'bring-up' system is necessary, which will also aid the Technical Manager in preparing his report for the management review.

10.6.11 *Site audit programme*

The Technical Manager should run through the forward audit programme for the site, which should specify department, date in terms of week commencing, and the auditor(s) concerned. It is helpful for auditors to work in pairs, certainly during their early audits, since two minds are better than one, and during the audit one auditor can ask the questions and the other can check that everything in the checklist is covered.

10.6.12 Review

The course should close with a review of the day, deal with any questions, remind the auditors that they will be accompanied by experienced auditors on their first audit, and that there will be a review meeting for everyone once the first series of audits has been completed.

10.6.13 First audits

The Technical Manager must recognize that it will be necessary for the auditors to be supported closely by him/herself or the consultant during all phases of the first audits they carry out, since they will be unfamiliar with the documentation, and will need to develop the confidence to ask awkward questions in unfamiliar departments.

10.6.14 Review and approved auditor status

Once all the auditors have carried out an audit, it will be prudent to convene a short review meeting for them all to compare experiences, ask for clarification, further explanation of the standard, etc.

When the Technical Manager is satisfied that the auditors are competent technically and, most importantly, have the right personal relationships and skills, then they should be deemed approved internal auditors and their names included in the schedule in the internal audit procedure.

10.7 Company awareness

Before the first internal audits take place the whole of the company needs to be briefed thoroughly, since the majority will have had little direct involvement in the project.

The briefing note, which ideally should be issued with the authority of the management review down the usual line management communication channels, should:

- summarize activity to date;
- emphasize the importance of constructive participation in the internal audit programme to:
  - (a) improve working practices
  - (b) ensure we 'Do what we say, say what we do, and have the records to prove it'
  - (c) achieve certification to BS EN ISO 9001;
- introduce the audit schedule.

NOTE: It cannot be emphasized too much that a successful internal audit programme is essential to the implementation of a successful quality management programme and certification to BS EN ISO 9001.

10.8 Summary

A successful internal audit programme is a prerequisite to certification to the standard. There needs to be:

- an established procedure comprising checklist, audit, review and corrective action, and close-out;
- a comprehensive training programme for the auditors;
- an internal audit schedule that requires frequent audits until the Technical Manager is satisfied the company is ready for assessment; thereafter every department should be audited at least twice a year;
- company awareness of the purpose of the programme and auditee knowledge of the part they play.

Internal quality audit

DO . . .

- ensure a clear audit procedure;
- give auditors a thorough training;
- keep to the audit schedule;
- be sure to keep track of corrective action and close it out,

DO NOT . . .

- forget to keep everyone in the company informed of their role in the audit programme;
- let the programme slip;
- assume that the auditors can cope;
- lose track of corrective action.

QFS   Quality Food Services

Document:	Company Procedure	Reference:	CP 001
		Issue:	1. 0
Title:	Procedure for Internal Audit	Date:	13-6-95
		Page:	1 of 2

Scope: This procedure applies to all audits carried out under the internal audit programme.

Purpose: To ensure that the management and execution of the internal audit programme is carried out in a consistent manner.

Responsibility: The Technical Manager is responsible for this procedure.

Procedure:

1. The Technical Manager will maintain an adequate number of approved internal auditors, whose names appear on the schedule attached to this procedure.
2. Every 6 months the Technical Manager will publish a schedule of audits for the coming 12 months, specifying the function /department to be audited, the week of the audit, and the auditors concerned.
3. The documentation for each audit will comprise:
   - the checklist, produced by the auditor before the audit
   - the nonconformance report, which defines the nonconformances found
   - the review meeting minutes, which summarize the corrective action and timescale agreed by the auditor, the Technical Manager and the management of the department concerned.
4. The Technical Manager will arrange follow-up audits to verify that corrective action has been implemented and has been effective.

Originated by: **Authorized by:**

Date: **Date:**

QFS   Quality Food Services

Document:	Company Procedure	**Reference:**	CP 006
		Issue:	1. 0
Title:	Procedure for Internal Audit	**Date:**	13-6-95
		Page:	2 of 2

Records

Schedule of approved auditors

Internal audit timetable and schedule

Internal audit checklist

Internal audit nonconformance report

Circulation

General Manager

Technical Manager

Departmental Managers

Originated by: **Authorized by:**

Date: **Date:**

QFS   Quality Food Services

Internal Audit Report – Audit Checklist

Subject:

Auditor(s):   **Date:**

_____
_____
_____
_____
_____
_____
_____
_____
_____
_____
_____
_____
_____
_____
_____
_____
_____
_____
_____
_____
_____
_____
_____
_____
_____
_____
_____
_____

Auditor:

Date:

QFS   Quality Food Services

Internal Audit Report – Nonconformance Report

Subject:

Auditor(s):   **Date:**

Auditor:

Date:

QFS   Quality Food Services

Internal Audit Report – Review Summary

Department:

Auditor(s):   **Date:**

Nonconformance (problem)	Action by:	Review date:	Completion date:

Auditor: **Auditee:**

Signed: **Signed:**

Date: **Date:**

11

Training

11.1 Introduction

In clause 4.18 the standard requires that personnel are adequately qualified to fulfil the jobs they do, that there are documented procedures to ensure that training needs are identified and met, and that records are kept to demonstrate that all employees have the necessary qualifications, training and experience to carry out the jobs they do. In looking at this area, assessors will require evidence that the staff they meet are appropriately trained.

Consideration needs to be given to the induction training when new employees join the company, general training needs, specific job training and the question of individual training records.

11.2 Induction training

Clearly, new employees should be given an adequate introduction to the business in the early weeks of their employment. In addition to the general matters of the history and objectives of the company, terms and conditions of employment, facilities, pension fund, etc., the introduction to a food company should include food legislation, hygiene regulations and an introduction to BS EN ISO 9001. These topics should be dealt with in a general way at induction, relative to the company activities, and very specific matters left to job induction in the department concerned.

11.2.1 Food hygiene

The broad requirements of the food hygiene regulations need to be summarized, namely:

- the company is a food business and has a legal responsibility in that respect;
- open food must be covered at the earliest opportunity;
- impeccable standards of housekeeping and hygiene are expected;
- overalls and headgear must be worn in production areas or wherever food is exposed;
- hands must be washed on entering production areas;
- waste must be managed responsibly;
- employees must report to the Medical Department after certain overseas holidays or visits;
- draw attention to particular technologies, e.g. meat processing, chilled/frozen products, where requirements are particularly stringent.

11.2.2 BS EN ISO 9001

New employees should be made aware that the company has/is working towards certification to the standard, and should be given a similar introduction to that received by the rest of the company. The message needs to convey:

- The Food Safety Act 1990 implemented into UK law the EEC Directive on the Official Control of Foodstuffs and introduced the 'Due Diligence' defence into UK legislation.
- Certification to BS EN ISO 9001, together with HACCP, Hazard Analysis of Critical Control Points, has become a recognized standard for acceptable quality management practice and thus can form the basis of capability to use the Due Diligence defence, if necessary. Indeed, many large companies and customers require this standard as a condition of business, so clearly it is in the company's interest to achieve and maintain the standard.
- Good practice and ISO 9001 require that all procedures and practices are documented and available to those who need them.

The principle is, as ever,

say what you do, do what you say, and have the records to prove it.

The Technical Manager should then explain the system fully, and point out that detailed procedures and work instructions relating to all jobs will be found in the documentation of the departments in which the new employees will work.

11.3 Job descriptions/work instructions

The expectation will be that all management and assistant management jobs will have a job description associated with them which
summarizes the responsibilities of the job, together with necessary
experience and qualifications. Annual appraisals are common, in
which performance is assessed, forward plans made and training
needs identified. Clerical and line operator tasks will generally be
specified in work instructions to be found in departmental documentation, and in these areas employees are generally able to carry
out many tasks. The simplest way of summarizing these capabilities
is with a matrix in each department – tasks across the top, names
down the side and ticks in the boxes as appropriate. The matrix is
completed and signed by departmental management, and reviewed
with the Personnel Department at least annually to identify training
needs and resource problems.

Such job-specific training is generally done within the department
by departmental management/trainers.

NOTE: When training records are being established in preparation
for certification, it is not necessary to repeat training already given.
It is perfectly satisfactory for a Departmental Manager to verify who
is competent to do what and create the record as the basis for future
action.

11.4 General training

Quite often general training is arranged, e.g. communication skills,
safety training, ISO 9001 awareness, etc., and in this case an entry in
each individual's record should be made.

11.5 Personal records

Personal records should exist for every employee, demonstrating
qualifications and capability. Thus at assessment, the assessors will ask
for the personal records of a selection of the people they meet during
the assessment, evidence of a formal annual review of training needs,
and confirmation that each department is adequately resourced with
an adequate number of staff with the requisite range of capability.

Evidence will be required that new staff, or staff engaged in tasks
they are not used to, are adequately supervised.

A model procedure can be found at the end of this chapter.

11.6 Summary

The essential requirements are that there is a trained workforce carrying out well-defined tasks. Thus the assessors will expect to find clear job descriptions and work instructions, a personal record for all employees indicating the skills they have, and assessment in each department of the skill resources required and possessed.

A training review should be conducted annually to define the forward training programme, with the objective of ensuring that the department/company has the right quantity and quality of resources, and that employees are properly prepared for future development.

Training

DO . . .

- be sure that everyone has a training record;
- ensure that all departments have an assessment of skills capability;
- ensure that there is an annual review of training requirements.

DO NOT . . .

- ignore these requirements;
- leave it to the last minute to prepare these records.

QFS   Quality Food Services

Document:	Company Procedure	Reference:	CP 015
		Issue:	1.0
Title:	Training	Date:	13-6-95
		Page:	1 of 2

Scope: This procedure applies to all training activities in the company.

Purpose: To ensure that all training needs are identified, implemented and recorded in order that the company has a trained and committed workforce.

Responsibility: This procedure is the responsibility of the Personnel Manager.

Procedure:

1. Induction training

   Induction training is provided for all new employees during the early weeks of their employment. The objective is to ensure that all new employees are integrated into the organization and become committed to the business. An awareness of the site is given together with knowledge of policies, products and structure. Emphasis is given to safety and hygiene, quality management policies and the commitment to BS EN ISO 9001.

2. Job training

   Job training is given to help each employee reach maximum efficiency as quickly as possible. Another employee will be assigned to give the necessary supervision, assistance and guidance until the employee is deemed to be proficient at the tasks required of him/her.

Originated by: **Authorized by:**

Date: **Date:**

QFS Quality Food Services

Document:	Company Procedure	**Reference:**	CP 015
		Issue:	1.0
Title:	Training	**Date:**	13-6-95
		Page:	2 of 2

3. Further training
   Further training is given to:

   (a) develop personnel to continuously seek performance improvement and to be adaptable and flexible to change;
   (b) to assist those suitable for promotion to take advantage of opportunities.

   The training needs are compiled into an annual training plan which is regularly reviewed and updated by Line Managers and the Personnel Manager.

4. Training records
   Records of all training undertaken are maintained to allow identification of individuals' capabilities and to monitor the effectiveness of training. Details of staff training are recorded and monitored by each department. Training records are stored in the Personnel Department for the duration of an individual's employment with the company.

Originated by: **Authorized by:**

Date: **Date:**

12

The assessment process

12.1 Introduction

There are several phases in the assessment process, which commences with the appointment of the assessors. Their first activity will be document review, when the documentation will be studied to verify that all clauses of the standard have been addressed and that the quality management system (QMS) is complete.

Note the principles of the assessor's judgement. Hold points are raised if there are serious deficiencies in the company system such that the principles of the standard are not being complied with. Immediate correction to an agreed timetable must be effected before certification can be recommended. If deficiencies are points of detail rather than principle, nonconformance notes are raised, with correction needed by the time of the assessor's next visit.

The first assessment will take place over several days to a specified programme, at the end of which there can be one of three possible results:

1. Serious deficiencies are found, such that significant parts of the standard have not been complied with. Hold points will be raised and the assessment repeated when corrective action has been implemented. Certification will not be recommended at this stage.
2. The standard will have been complied with, but minor points of detail will be lacking. Nonconformance notes will be raised, to be corrected by the next surveillance visit. Certification to the standard will be recommended.
3. No problems found. Certification to the standard will be recommended.

Subsequent to the successful assessment, the assessors will typically return every six months for five surveillance visits, at which hold points or nonconformance notes could be raised. Hold points will have to be corrected quickly to an agreed timescale if certification is to be retained.

On the sixth visit the full assessment may be repeated.

12.2 Appointment of assessors

Thought needs to be given in plenty of time with regard to which assessment company to use. They all have busy schedules and it is sensible to ask for quotations at least 6 months before the anticipated date in order to pencil in a date in the chosen company's diary. Generally, a sensible time to do this is when the first draft of documentation is complete and training of the internal audit team is starting. This will give ample time for the audit programme to get under way and an adequate quantity of quality records to be assembled. Assessors like to have at least 3 months worth of quality records available to them.

A list of assessment companies is contained in Appendix B, and it is sensible to ask for quotations from two or three. Apart from price, companies should be asked for a specification for their activities, a draft timescale, and a summary of their experience in your sector of the food industry. Although an assessment house ought to be able to operate anywhere, it is an advantage if they have food industry experience, preferably in your area, since it will be easier for the assessor to follow the technology involved. Expect to be asked to provide a summary of your company activities, a draft scope, and indications of the size of the business, i.e. turnover, number of people employed, number of sites, number of product types, etc.

Once the assessment house has been appointed, it is sensible to keep them in touch with progress, particularly if it becomes necessary to adjust the date of document review.

12.3 Document review

The purpose of document review is to demonstrate to the assessor that all clauses of the standard have been addressed by the documentation and that a comprehensive quality management system (QMS) is in place.

Document review generally takes no more than a day, and everyone in the business, and particularly the Gatehouse and Reception, should be aware that it is taking place. An office needs to be provided for the assessor, in which should be placed a copy of the company documentation; and protective clothing should be available. Arrangements for refreshments should be made in accordance with the assessor's wishes.

The format of the day will be:

1. Opening meeting, attended by the assessor, the management team of the site and the Document Controller. The assessor will explain his/her intentions, ask for a factory tour, define the reporting mechanisms and discuss any points anyone wishes to raise.
2. Site/factory tour – the purpose of this is to familiarize the assessor with the activities, technology and layout of the factory, in order that he/she can better relate to the documentation.
3. Inspection of documentation – the assessor will spend the bulk of the day examining the documentation, following audit trails through it, etc. to verify that the QMS is complete and that all clauses of the standard have been addressed. The Technical Manager and/or the Document Controller should be available as necessary to answer any queries the assessor may have, and to agree any hold points or nonconformances that are identified.
4. Closing meeting – attended by those at the opening meeting. The assessor will agree or revise the scope of the assessment, i.e. what it is that the company will be certified for, and explain any hold points or nonconformances that are raised. If hold points have been raised, a date for repeat document review will be agreed, and if nonconformances are raised, dates for the assessment will be agreed, by which time the nonconformances will have to be corrected.

The results of document review should be communicated throughout the company.

12.4 The assessment

Several weeks before the assessment the lead assessor will provide a programme and timetable for the assessment. It is quite likely that in medium to large companies an assessment team of several people might be involved. In this case arrangements should be made for somebody to accompany each assessor at all times to ensure the assessor gets the answers to questions asked, finds his/her way round the site, particularly when following audit trails, and to agree hold points or nonconformances when they are found.

The programme should be made known to everyone in the company by means of a briefing through normal Line Management channels. The briefing should cover:

- the dates of the assessment overall and the date and time of the assessment of each department, i.e. the total programme;
- the identification of the departmental host who will accompany the assessor in the department;

- advice to answer only the question asked and not to tender information the assessor might be thought to want to hear;
- advice to answer confidently – the job holder knows more about the job than the assessor!

The format of the assessment will be similar to that for document review, in that there will be an opening meeting; the assessment, during which there will be a daily review; and, finally, the closing meeting.

1. The opening meeting will follow the pattern of that held at the document review, i.e. it should be attended by the management team plus the Document Controller. The lead assessor will review the programme and make any necessary adjustments, discuss the reporting format, agree domestic arrangements and answer any questions. Obviously, the company will have arranged that all activities falling within the scope of the assessment will be taking place during the assessment.
2. The assessment will then proceed according to the programme, the assessors operating from office accommodation reserved for them. At the end of each day the assessors will review their findings with the Technical Manager and anyone else who wishes to be present, and at the beginning of each day will discuss the day's activities, in particular any changes that need to be made in the light of previous progress and findings. At the end of the assessment the assessors will need time to summarize their findings, complete the paperwork and prepare for the closing meeting.
3. The closing meeting should be attended by the management team and anyone else deemed appropriate. The lead assessor will summarize his/her findings, which will have been agreed with the Technical Manager during the assessment and are therefore not a matter for debate, and will indicate whether he/she can recommend certification. If there are hold points, this will not be the case and a date will be agreed by which corrective action will have been carried out and seen to be effective, such that the assessors can return and hopefully sign them off as complete. If only a few nonconformances have been found, the assessor will indicate that certification to the standard can be recommended. In either case, the formal paperwork will be signed by both parties and a copy left with the company as a formal quality record.
4. The assessors' paperwork and report will be reviewed by the management of the assessment house and if all is well certification to the standard will be awarded. Generally the certificate will arrive within a month of assessment.

12.5 Surveillance visits

Subsequent to certification, the assessors will return by appointment, typically every 6 months, to verify that adherence to the standard is being maintained. At the start of each visit the assessors will automatically examine the minutes of the management review, the document control records, and the internal audit reports. In this way they can quickly become aware of changes to the QMS, any action taken by management and details of current problems, and thus focus their activities on anything they deem to be necessary. They will also audit in depth a proportion of the company activity, which will have been identified in the paperwork of the previous visit. The reporting format and consequences of any findings are as at the assessment.

12.6 Summary

This chapter has described the procedure, format and reporting mechanism of the whole assessment process and should enable the reader to be well prepared for assessment.

Assessment

DO . . .

- appoint an assessment house with experience relevant to your activities;
- ensure that everyone is aware that document review and assessment are happening and that all arrangements are complete;
- make sure that all activities included in the scope of the assessment are taking place during the assessment;
- put in place thorough arrangements for the facilities, needs and comfort of the assessors during their visits.

DO NOT . . .

- underestimate the thoroughness of the assessors;
- allow visitors on document review and assessment days.

13

Achievement of the standard – what next?

13.1 Introduction

So we have arrived at a situation where the certificate has been achieved, celebration quite rightly has been enjoyed, and it might be thought that apart from maintaining the practices and satisfying the surveillance assessments, there is nothing more to be done. A common error, when in reality achievement of the ISO 9001 certificate gives the company a system to be used and built upon, leading to exciting possibilities – namely progression to total quality management (TQM) practices. **The time has come to use the system to the benefit of all.**

In this chapter we consider the total quality management philosophy, and take a look at the issue of measurement and performance, quality costs, quality improvement activities, teamworking and communication.

13.2 Total quality management

Oakland in his book *Total Quality Management* (1989) has defined TQM as 'an approach to improving the effectiveness and flexibility of business as a whole' and being 'concerned with moving the focus of control from outside the individual to within; the objective being to make everyone accountable for their own performance, and to get them committed to attaining quality in a highly motivated fashion' and 'concerned chiefly with changing attitudes and skills so that the culture of the organisation becomes one of preventing failure and the norm is operating right first time.'

An effective TQM programme comprises a healthy mixture of:

- clear quality policy;
- effective organization for quality management;
- good understanding of performance indices and quality costs;
- appropriate use of computers, statistical process control, problem-solving techniques, benchmarking, quality improvement teams and quality circles;
- an environment that encourages continuous improvement, so that everyone has the intention to satisfy their customers' needs;
- effective and continuous communication.

Achievement of certification to BS EN ISO 9001 will have done a lot to contribute to this. Undoubtedly management commitment will have been demonstrated through a clear quality policy, a management structure properly resourced to implement the preferred procedures, and appropriate review procedures to ensure that corrective action has been implemented effectively. The whole being designed to understand the customer want and to deliver the customer need.

But there are several ways in which the system can be sharpened up. An understanding of quality costs in association with line performance details can identify problem areas and prioritize corrective action. Various analytical tools such as flow charts, Pareto diagrams, cause and effect charts and brainstorming can be used to identify and quantify the cause of problems and then produce solutions. Benchmarking techniques will enable a judgement to be made about performance in comparison with competitors and industry norms. Computers can be used to improve process control and data handling, supported where appropriate by SPC – statistical process control.

Use of quality improvement teams and quality circles not only addresses problems but also encourages collective responsibility amongst all to pursue the cult of continuous improvement. They also engender a feeling of empowerment that individuals can get things done. Finally, thorough, well-applied training will ensure that corrective action is effective.

So let us look at these matters.

13.3 Performance indices and quality costs

Normal management information will expose some problem areas, e.g. line efficiencies, waste, reject product in production, supplier timeliness, quantity and quality, prompt invoicing and payment in accounts, etc., but an understanding of the cost of quality will give an organization a different perspective of its operation and will contribute to a deeper understanding of the source of cost.

However, it must be recognized that to do this thoroughly involves an approach that is different from usual accounting practice and therefore resource needs to be allocated to it – and not just accounting resource. A small multidisciplinary team is appropriate to identify salary and wage costs, cost of materials and equipment, costs of inefficiency, etc.

What are quality costs? They have been discussed thoroughly by Groocock (1974) and are defined as the costs of failure, appraisal and prevention and are detailed in Table 13.1.

The costs of failure are those associated with everything that goes wrong both inside and outside the company, i.e. they involve relationships with customers, suppliers and enforcement bodies. And the costs of putting things right should be included.

The costs of appraisal are the costs of verifying that all is well, i.e. the costs of checking correctness, and the costs of prevention are the costs of planning quality, its implementation and maintenance, i.e. the costs of designing-in quality and designing-out the cause of failure.

Having identified the costs of quality, the management art is to judge their acceptability. The name of the game is not eliminating quality costs but judging their acceptability. Appropriate costs of prevention should be incurred to design quality in, and the costs of appraisal should be adequate to verify that the quality management

Table 13.1 Quality costs

(a) Failure	
Internal	*External*
Waste	Supplier management
Rework	Repair
Scrap	Warranty
Re-inspection	Complaints
Downgrading	Returns
High stocks	Liability

Plus the costs of analysis and corrective action

(b) Appraisal – the cost of checking correctness, i.e. is it right?
Inspection
Audits
Inspection equipment
Vendor rating

(c) Prevention – design, implementation, maintenance
Product/service requirements
Quality planning
Quality assurance
Inspection equipment
Training
Miscellaneous

system is working satisfactorily. But costs of failure need to be assessed diligently, prioritized and corrective action instituted, and that is a job for the management review group as it supervises corrective action taken to deal with nonconformances found by the internal audit programme (Chapter 10). The resources necessary for corrective action for both programmes will need to be controlled and priorities decided. Indeed, in some cases quality improvement teams may be established, and some problems may be given to quality circles to address (see below).

13.4 Quality improvement teams and quality circles

As the internal audit programme and the quality cost assessment mature, so problem areas will be identified and suggestions for improvement will emerge from audit review meetings, and discussions about the quality costs. Management may decide to tackle these items by establishing quality improvement teams and/or by setting up a quality circles programme.

13.4.1 Quality improvement teams

Quality improvement teams are appointed by management to address specific problems. A leader is appointed together with the necessary multidisciplinary team members, terms of reference are provided, and a reporting date is specified. The team uses its knowledge and experience, together with any of the quality tools described below. When the recommendations have been accepted and implemented, the team is stood down. In this way the nonconformances and problem areas can be tackled in a structured way.

13.4.2 Quality circles

On the other hand, there will be a level of issues that are best identified, prioritized and addressed by the employees themselves, which is a situation in which quality circles are appropriate.

Quality circles are 'groups of people doing similar work who meet regularly, in normal working hours, to identify, analyse and solve work-related problems, and recommend solutions to management'.

The quality circles programme will be supervised by a Facilitator, who is responsible for setting up the circles, training the leaders, nurturing the circle activity and co-ordinating the programme. He or she may well come from the Quality Assurance Department, and will train the circles in the techniques they will use, namely:

- identifying problems through use of brainstorming and cause and effect analysis;
- quantifying problems through data collection:
  (a) recording using checksheets, measles diagrams, histograms, control charts;
  (b) displaying results, using bar charts, graphs, pie charts, histograms, Pareto charts;
- generating solutions;
- presentational skills – to present results and solutions.

13.5 Quality tools

1. Computers: it goes without saying that computers can be used in all aspects of quality management – process control, quality records and data processing. Remember to validate the applications to demonstrate that calculations are correct.
2. Statistical process control (SPC) – this is applied in two main ways, acceptance sampling and control of process variables. Oakland (1986) and Hubbard (1990) have written excellent books on the subject.
3. Techniques:
   - Brainstorming – carried out in a group about a given topic. Several simple rules: move in turn round the group, one idea per turn; if no idea, pass; no criticism; no discussion until end. Then collate into possible projects, classify as circle controllable, part circle controllable, and not circle controllable.
   - Cause and effect analysis – possible causes of problems are considered under the headings of Men, Machines, Materials and Methods. Causes are ranked in order of relevance to the problem and addressed accordingly.
   - Data collection and presentation – record sheets, checksheets, bar charts, graphs, pie charts, histograms.
   - Benchmarking – company practice and performance is compared with that of similar companies and industry norms.

13.6 The cult of continuous improvement

So there is in place a quality management system of ISO 9001 pedigree, an appreciation of quality costs and an aggressive approach to identifying, quantifying and solving problems. Management must ensure that this capability is put to good use and that the cult of continuous improvement is encouraged and developed by consistent leadership and action that demonstrates commitment to quality. Effective COMMUNICATION must ensure that all are aware of their responsibility, are aware of what is going on, and know the results.

Management must continually emphasize:

- the need to understand customer requirement;
- that processes must be defined and observed to meet this need;
- awareness of quality costs;
- identification on nonconformance and performance indicators;
- the importance of effective corrective action.

Best wishes for an effective quality management system!

14

Other accreditation/certification systems

14.1 Introduction

Other standards, codes of practice, etc. have been referred to earlier in this book, and it would not be complete without more on this subject. These may be complementary or supplementary to ISO 9000 series requirements – there is an awareness requirement with regard to legislative compliance and existence of relevant guidance – or may be 'free-standing', operating entirely without reference elsewhere other than the need to comply with the law.

The message from this chapter is that wherever you are, you should seek out through trade bodies, enforcement authorities, government and other appropriate sources of information whether or not schemes or standards exist that may have some bearing on your own systems, methodology or products. This done, they should be critically reviewed to determine whether or not they are relevant to your business and, if so, whether or not you wish to seek compliance with them. If you are commencing to seek ISO certification, it is clearly most efficacious to address any other compliance needs at the same time to save duplication of effort, paperwork, record keeping, etc.

14.2 Industry schemes

A number of voluntary schemes are in place in the UK which require adherence to standards or codes by members of trade associations. Some of these are almost completely self-regulated, and others involve use of third-party auditors, assessors or inspectors. Some examples of these are given below, and contact points for further information are provided at the end of the chapter.

14.2.1 British Meat Manufacturers' Association (BMMA)

BMMA operate an Accredited Standards Scheme and the Charter Quality Bacon Scheme.

The Accredited Standards Scheme consists of a series of standards to which members are required to adhere. Subjects covered are:

- standard for meat raw materials used in meat products
- standard for the hygienic and safe manufacture, storage and distribution of meat and other food products;
- standard for acceptable levels of pork rind and other collagenous material in meat products;
- standard for the use of additives in meat products and products containing meat;
- standard for the clear and informative labelling of meat products;
- standard for the production of bacon and bacon joints;
- advice notes for labelling of cured meats;
- code of practice on composition of meat pastes;
- standard for Hazard Analysis and Critical Control Points.

The Charter Quality Bacon Scheme exists to ensure the consistent high quality of all types of bacon products, and the requirements are:

1. compliance with the operating manual and the quality manual which cover products, processing, curing, hygiene, temperature control, housekeeping and structural finish;
2. adherence to the Accredited Standards;
3. satisfactory reports from the Meat and Livestock Commission Quality Assurance team, who inspect six times per year, and satisfactory review by the Charter Bacon Executive.

A Charter Ham Scheme and a Farm Assurance Scheme are also operated.

14.2.2 British Frozen Food Federation (BFFF)

BFFC operate a Frozen Food Accreditation Scheme relating to the manufacture and quality assurance of frozen products. Topics covered are fabrication, plant and machinery, pest and rodent control, personnel hygiene, site hygiene, raw material control, process control, management and customer complaints.

14.3 National and international schemes

14.3.1 Standards Association of Zimbabwe

The Standards Association of Zimbabwe has adopted the ISO 9000 series of standards and published it as SAZS ISO 9000.

14.3.2 European Foundation for Quality Management – self-assessment for total quality management

In 1988 leading West European businesses recognized the competitive advantages of developing a quality edge, and formed the European Foundation for Quality Management, with the objective of:

- accelerating the acceptance of quality as a strategy for global competitive advantage;
- stimulating and assisting the deployment of quality improvement activities.

The guidelines for self-assessment (European Foundation for Quality Management, 1994) argue that self-assessment offers several benefits:

- the identification of progress against a model for business excellence;
- a sound detailed basis for consideration of strategic direction and prioritizing future improvement activities;
- it energizes people and teams to pursue excellence;
- it reinforces the link between enabling activities and excellence in business results;
- it provides the basis for benchmarking against other organizations.

The self-assessment cycle involves:

- developing commitment;
- planning the cycle;
- establishing model and reporting systems;
- communicating plans;
- educating staff;
- conducting self-assessment;
- establishing action plans;
- implementing action plans;
- reviewing progress.

Areas addressed are leadership, policy and strategy, people management, resources, processes, customer satisfaction, people satisfaction, impact on society, and business results.

14.3.3 *New Zealand Q-Base programme*

An interesting development in New Zealand is the Q-Base code of practice, devised as an 'entry level' quality system for small businesses for whom the full ISO system would be daunting, but who wanted to develop a sound base quality system from which the full system could be developed when needed. It is also intended to provide a company wlth some of the economic pay-back that comes from 'right first time'. The code covers the following:

- responsibility and authority;
- documentation control;
- training and work instructions;
- inspection plans;
- inspection equipment;
- inspection status and control of nonconforming material;
- quality records.

At present there are 1610 companies in New Zealand certified to ISO standards, and 252 companies that have the Q-Base standard, with another 223 applications being processed. The Q-Base pro- gramme is operational in Australia, Canada, Sweden and Vietnam, and licences are being developed in Indonesia, the Philippines, Malaysia, Singapore, New Caledonia and Japan.

Full details can be found in Appendix E.

14.4 Guidelines and codes of practice

14.4.1 *IFST guidelines to good manufacturing practice*

The Institute of Food Science and Technology (UK) produced a guide to GMP in 1987, now in its 3rd edition. Its full title is *Food and Drink – Good Manufacturing Practice: A Guide to its Responsible Management* and it is referred to in some of the guidance notes on the ISO standard. While not seeking to invent the wheel, it does deal with the principles involved in GMP and does offer guidance in areas where none may be readily available. The IFST guide has been popularly received in many situations, and parts now form the basis of some commercial contracts, have been referred to in civil law cases, and a substantial amount has been taken up by the New Zealand IFST in liaison with the New Zealand Ministry of Food to provide the basis of a guide of their own.

14.4.2 IFST listing of codes

Another IFST publication is a *Listing of Codes of Practice Applicable to Foods,* which was produced by an IFST/MAFF project with sponsorship from MAFF. Although neither endorsing nor vouching for the validity of any of them, the publication presents a range of codes of practice and similar documents that were identified up to the time of publication in 1993, and may therefore provide a useful reference point for those seeking to know if a particular topic was covered by such codes up to that time.

14.5 Codex Alimentarius

The Codex Alimentarius Commission is a body set up to establish minimum standards for international trade. It is intended that compliance with Codex requirements should safeguard the integrity of the food in question, and preclude trade barriers preventing its entry to any participating country. The standards are agreed, under the auspices of FAO\WHO, through a laborious and lengthy sequence of negotiation between participating countries, with one acting as a lead body.

There are now numerous Codex standards covering such diverse matters as a Code for Ante- and Post-mortem Inspection of Slaughter Animals (CAC|RPC 12-197 FAO/WHO, 1979) to a Code of Hygienic Practice for the processing of frogs' legs (CAC/RCP 30-1983, FAO/WHO).

14.6 Confidence marks

These days it is often not good enough to provide a simple answer like 'Yes' to the question 'Is it kosher?' or 'gluten free' or 'nut free', or whatever. The consumer is ever more likely to want some sort of proof or evidence that it is indeed so, while the check-out operative may well be best advised from a legal stance to reply 'I'm sorry, I really don't know' and let the matter be referred to a higher authority. Problems of this sort are partly resolved by the use of marking schemes whereby the mark confirms that the product has been made to certain prescribed standards or prepared from prescribed materials.

Examples of such schemes include:

- vegetarian – allows the use of a symbol where the requirements of the Vegetarian Society are met (in the UK);
- vegan – similar to the above with stricter controls on ingredients;
- organic – allows 'organic' description/claims – supervised in the UK by the Soil Association (covered by EEC legislation);

- gluten-free – in the UK the Coeliac Society endorses the use of a symbol when no wheat gluten is present;
- kosher – applied to foods in accordance with Jewish religious requirements;
- halal – complying with Muslim requirements for slaughter, etc.;

and various others.

14.7 Distributors' own brands and contracts

Most distributors' own brand (DOB) products, also referred to as 'own label' products, are produced by third-party packers against very specific standards. The majority of the brand owners conduct technical audits of their suppliers at regular intervals and/or use third-party auditors for this purpose. We have said earlier that ISO 9001 certification can assist in reducing the depth of audit in the quality systems area and minimize duplication of effort where one producer is manufacturing for several DOBs.

Multiple retailers such as Marks & Spencer, J. Sainsbury, Albert Heine, Safeway, Tesco, Asda, Carrefour, etc. often have their own standards and/or cross refer to others including parts of the ISO standards. It is thus possible to encounter a requirement to meet ISO standard components without there being a requirement to hold the certification itself.

14.8 In conclusion

If there are other standards and schemes, existing or planned, which might be included in future editions that readers may be aware of, we should be pleased to hear of them.

14.9 Contact addresses

British Frozen Food Federation, 2nd Floor, Barclays Bank Chambers, 55 High Street, Grantham, Lincs NG31 6NE, UK.

British Meat Manufacturers' Association, 19 Cornwall Terrace, London NW1 4QP, UK.

Food and Drink Federation, 6 Catherine Street, London WC2B 5JJ, UK.

Institute of Food Science and Technology (UK), 5 Cambridge Court, 210 Shepherd's Bush Road, London W6 7NJ, UK.

The Soil Association, Symbol Scheme, Organic Marketing Company Ltd, 86 Colston Street, Bristol, BS51 5BB, UK.

Appendix A

Model quality manual: QFS Quality Food Services

QFS Quality Food Services

Document:	Quality Manual	Reference:	QM
		Issue:	1.0
Title:	1 Contents, Index	Date:	13-6-95
	and Distribution	Page:	1 of 3

Contents

1. Contents index and distribution list

2. Amendment procedure and records

3. Management policy statement

4. Scope of activity

5. Management organization and responsibility

6. Management review of quality system

7. Document control policy

8. Contract review

9. Manufacturing control

    (a)   Introduction

        • material specification and product formulae

        • production planning

    (b)   Production control

    (c)   Special processes

    (d)   Production records

    (e)   Hygiene procedures

    (f)   Finished product testing

10. Purchasing

11. Customer-supplied product

12. Product identification and traceability

13. Inspection and testing

14. Inspection, measuring and test equipment

15. Inspection, measuring and test status

Originated by:

Date:

Authorized by:

Date:

QFS   Quality Food Services

Document:	Quality Manual	Reference:	QM
		Issue:	1.0
Title:	1 Contents, Index	Date:	13-6-95
	and Distribution	Page:	2 of 3

16. Control of nonconforming materials, work-in-progress and finished product

17. Corrective action

18. Handling, storage, packaging, preservation and delivery

19. Quality management

20. Laboratory

21. Quality records

22. Internal quality audit

23. Training

24. Statistical techniques

25. Index of company procedures

26. Index of departmental manuals

Originated by: **Authorized by:**

Date: **Date:**

QFS   Quality Food Services

Document:	Quality Manual	**Reference:**	QM
		Issue:	1. 0
Title:	1 Contents, Index	**Date:**	13-6-95
	and Distribution	**Page:**	3 of 3

Distribution

(a) Controlled copies

Quality Manager – Master copy

General Manager

Distribution Manager

Manufacturing Manager

Personnel Manager

Engineering Manager

Commercial Manager

Production Plant – lines A to C

Production Plant – lines D to H

(b) Uncontrolled copies

All requests for uncontrolled copies shall be directed to the Quality Manager and must be authorized by the General Manager.

Uncontrolled copies will only be issued to agencies outside the company, and will be marked 'Uncontrolled'.

A record of issue will be maintained by the Quality Manager.

Originated by: **Authorized by:**

Date: **Date:**

QFS   Quality Food Services

Document:	Quality Manual	Reference:	QM
		Issue:	1.0
Title:	2 Amendments Procedure	Date:	13-6-95
	and Records	Page:	1 of 1

Amendments procedure

1. Every page of a controlled document shall be authorized, dated and carry a revision status, comprising an issue number and revision number, e.g. 2.1. Every amendment will be implemented through issue of revised page(s) which will similarly be authorized, dated and carry a revision number.

2. All amendments to the quality manual will be authorized by the General Manager and issued by the Technical Manager.

3. All amendments to controlled documents will be authorized by the appropriate manager and issued by the Technical Manager. A copy of obsolete documents will be retained by the Technical Manager.

4. Authorized amendments will be filed in the appropriate copies of manuals/procedures by the responsible person in each department. Old copies will be destroyed.

Amendment records

1. A record of all changes made to documentation will be retained by the Technical Manager.

2. These records will be retained for 5 years.

3. Procedure CP1 refers.

Originated by:

Date:

Authorized by:

Date:

QFS   *Quality Food Services*

Document:	Quality Manual	Reference:	QM
		Issue:	1.0
Title:	3 Management Policy	Date:	13-6-95
	Statement	Page:	1 of 1

The company produces quality products for sale on world markets.

Through a policy of continuous quality improvements we are committed to achieving and maintaining the highest standards for product safety and, within a cost profile agreed with our customers, world class standards for product quality and customer service. In partnership with our suppliers, our customers and our employees we are working towards a goal of total consumer satisfaction.

As evidence of our commitment we will pursue, obtain and hold certification to BS EN ISO 9001.

Originated by: **Authorized by:**

Date: **Date:**

QFS Quality Food Services

Document:	Quality Manual	Reference:	QM
		Issue:	1.0
Title:	4 Scope of activity	Date:	13-6-95
		Page:	1 of 1

This section should contain a summary of:

- company activities and products;
- the departments in which they are carried out;
- the main equipment used.

Originated by: **Authorized by:**

Date: **Date:**

QFS   Quality Food Services

Document:	Quality Manual	**Reference:**	QM
		Issue:	1.0
Title:	5 Management Organization	**Date:**	13-6-95
	and Responsibility	**Page:**	1 of 3

1. Management structure

The structure of the management team is summarized in the attached organization chart.

- The General Manager is responsible for:
  - the effective management of all resources, and timely achievement of agreed production output plans to within predefined quality and cost standards;
  - ensuring organization is appropriate to company objectives;
  - ensuring that effective communication channels internal and external to the site and across functions are established and maintained;
  - a major contribution to establishing company policy and ensuring effective and consistent operation;
  - the development of the manufacturing strategy and its effective implementation.
- The Manufacturing Manager is responsible for:
  - achieving an agreed production plan;
  - meeting product quality standards;
  - achieving target production costs;
  - ensuring manufacturing procedures are observed;
  - maximum usage of machine capability and labour availability.
- The Technical Manager is responsible for:
  - receipt and storage of raw and packaging materials,
  - timely supply of materials to production;
  - setting and auditing of line quality standards;
  - recording and storage of statutory weight management information;
  - laboratory management;
  - implementation and maintenance of vendor assurance programmes;
  - audit of production processes, hygiene procedures, and finished product quality standards;
  - development and commissioning of new products and processes;
  - establishment and maintenance of the BS EN ISO 9001 programme;
- The Engineering Manager is responsible for:
  - performance of plant and machinery to defined standards;
  - planned maintenance and overhaul of plant and machinery;
  - selection, purchase and installation of new machinery;
  - design and workshop services;

Originated by:	**Authorized by:**
Date:	**Date:**

QFS   Quality Food Services

Document:	Quality Manual	Reference:	QM
		Issue:	1.0
Title:	5 Management Organization	Date:	13-6-95
	and Responsibility	Page:	2 of 3

Engineering Manager (cont.)
  – site services and building maintenance;
  – statutory plant records and safety inspections;
  – engineering stores;
  – training and development of engineering staff;
  – management of contractors (approved contractors scheme).
• The Personnel and Administration Manager is responsible for:
  – advice regarding recruitment, remuneration, training, safety, communication, etc.;
  – recruitment of new staff;
  – development of formal consultation systems with employees;
  – negotiating terms and conditions.
• The Commercial Manager is responsible for:
  – accounts payable;
  – fixed asset register;
  – provision of management information.
• The Distribution Manager is responsible for:
  – warehousing and distribution of materials and finished goods;
  – management of transport.
• The Projects Manager is responsible for:
  – management of major building and engineering projects.
• The Production Manager is responsible for:
  – supporting the Manufacturing Manager with regard to special manufacturing projects.

2. BS EN ISO 9001
  Responsibility for management of the BS EN ISO 9001 programme is delegated through the General Manager to the Technical Manager. The General Manager will hold a review of the BS EN ISO 9001 system twice a year.

Originated by:		Authorized by:
Date:		Date:

QFS   Quality Food Services

Document:	Quality Manual	**Reference:**	QM
		Issue:	1.0
Title:	5 Management Organization	**Date:**	13-6-95
	and Responsibility	**Page:**	3 of 3

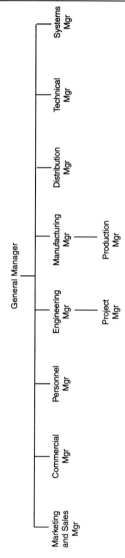

Originated by: **Authorized by:**

Date: **Date:**

QFS Quality Food Services

Document:	Quality Manual	Reference:	QM
		Issue:	1.0
Title:	6 Management Review	Date:	13-6-95
		Page:	1 of 1

The General Manager will hold a formal review of the effectiveness of the BS EN ISO 9001 quality management system twice a year.

The agenda will include:

- review of quality policy;

- review of external audit reports;

- review of internal audit programme;

- document control;

- vendor assurance programme;

- nonconforming product;

- complaint review;

- quality performance.

The minutes will identify the person responsible for corrective action, and the completion date.

Originated by: **Authorized by:**

Date: **Date:**

QFS *Quality Food Services*

Document:	Quality Manual	Reference:	QM
		Issue:	1.0
Title:	7 Document Control	Date:	13-6-95
	Policy	Page:	1 of 1

1. The Document control policy relevant to the BS EN ISO 9001 quality management system is based upon:

   - company quality policy
   - company quality manual and company procedures
   - departmental manuals and procedures

2. All documents are widely available to all who need them in support of the effective functioning of the quality management system. They will be issued as controlled documents: uncontrolled copies will only be issued externally, and then with the express permission of the General Manager.

3. The Technical Manager is responsible for document control of all documents. The control mechanism is defined in company procedure CP 001 – Procedure for Document Control.

4. Company procedures will be prepared in accord with procedure CP 002 – Procedure for Preparing Procedures.

5. Departmental manuals and procedures will be prepared in accordance with CP 003 – Procedure for Preparing Departmental Manuals and Procedures.

Originated by: **Authorized by:**

Date: **Date:**

QFS   Quality Food Services

Document:	Quality Manual	Reference:	QM
		Issue:	1.0
Title:	8 Contract Review	Date:	13-6-95
		Page:	1 of 1

The responsibility for contract review rests with Sales and Marketing Departments. It is the responsibility of the Technical Manager to respond to requests for new activity, and to prepare the appropriate specifications.

Implementation of agreed requests will be in accord with CP 027 – Design and Development of New Products.

Originated by:	Authorized by:
Date:	Date:

QFS   Quality Food Services

Document:	Quality Manual	**Reference:**	QM
		Issue:	1.0
Title:	9 Manufacturing Control	**Date:**	13-6-95
		Page:	1 of 3

1. Introduction

The basis of the manufacturing operation is receipt of materials, product formulations and specifications, and agreement to the production plan.

1.1 Material specifications and product formulations

These are issued in accord with CP 027 – Design and Development of New Products.

1.2 Production planning

Each period, the Planning Group updates the production plans based on a revised Sales and Marketing forecast.

The General Manager, Manufacturing Manager and Planner agree the plans that are the basis of the production commitment. The factory plan is reviewed weekly on a rolling basis, being firm 1 week ahead, and estimated 1 month ahead against a capacity review.

The Purchasing Department schedules the raw and packaging material deliveries in time slots in line with these plans.

Programmes are agreed 1 week in advance between the Planning Group and the Manufacturing Manager. In general no change to the weekly plan is accepted during the week in question. The weekly production plan is communicated to the Production Groups using the production plan form.

2. Production control

Company objectives require that production is carried out to the required volume, with consistent achievement of the specified quality standard, at a target cost in timely manner.

To achieve these objectives, production is managed in accordance with the following policies:

• All ingredients and packaging materials are received as good. They may be

Originated by:	**Authorized by:**
Date:	**Date:**

QFS   Quality Food Services

Document:	Quality Manual	Reference:	QM
		Issue:	1.0
Title:	9 Manufacturing Control	Date:	13-6-95
		Page:	2 of 3

subject to inspection and testing at the discretion of the Technical Manager. Procedures for sampling and testing are defined in procedure CP 004 – Sampling

- Product and packaging formats issued by the Technical Department in accordance with development procedures.
- Manufacturing operations must be carried out in accordance with the appropriate departmental manuals and procedures. The procedures for monitoring and control of quality during manufacture will be defined in the production manuals – Quality Procedures.
- Finished products must meet the product quality standards set.
- Management of all factory trials will be controlled by the Technical Manager according to procedure CP 025 – Management of Factory Trials.
- The Technical Department will regularly audit operating procedures (CP 006) and the quality of finished products (CP 020) to verify that standards are being achieved, and to resolve any problems that may arise.
- Issue of all documents to BS EN ISO 9001 standards will be carried out before production commences. The Technical Manager may issue concession notes with draft specifications or procedures to cover trial or commissioning work.

3. Special processes
   All processes can be verified by subsequent inspection and testing of the product.

4. Production records
   Production records relating to any finished or intermediate product should clearly identify product, date and any other relevant data identified in the plant manual.

   Specified production records should be kept for a period equivalent to the shelf-life of the product to assist in product traceability and product liability.

Originated by:	Authorized by:
Date:	Date:

QFS   Quality Food Services

Document:	Quality Manual	**Reference:**	QM
		Issue:	1.0
Title:	9 Manufacturing Control	**Date:**	13-6-95
		Page:	3 of 3

The production manual will specify the detail of records and frequency of recording.

5. Hygienic procedures

5.1 Cleaning procedures

These will be specified in the appropriate production manual.

5.2 Hygiene and housekeeping audit procedures

The state of cleanliness of all production areas will be audited by the Technical Department.

Audit results will be summarized and presented to production management.

6. Finished product testing

Company policy is to operate a quality assurance system, whereby on-line controls are carried out by trained operators to ensure the achievement of required standards.

In addition, packed stock audits are carried out and the results reported to management.

Originated by: **Authorized by:**

Date: **Date:**

QFS   Quality Food Services

Document:	Quality Manual	Reference:	QM
		Issue:	1.0
Title:	10 Purchasing	Date:	13-6-95
		Page:	1 of 1

All raw and packaging materials used in the company will have been purchased by the Purchasing Department according to procedures CP 012 – Generation and Placement of orders – and CP 013 – Selection and Approval of suppliers.

Materials are accepted for use following examination in accordance with procedure CP 004 – Sampling.

The performance of suppliers will be appraised according to procedure CP 014 – Assessment of Supplier Performance. Supplier performance will be reviewed at the biannual supplier contact meetings.

Quality-related services, e.g. calibration, pest control, etc. will be supported by a technical specification which defines:

- the service, including acceptable tolerances where appropriate;
- a nominated company employee to be responsible for the service;
- a record system to demonstrate that the responsible employee has verified that the service concerned has been provided within the targets and tolerances specified.

Originated by: **Authorized by:**

Date: **Date:**

QFS   Quality Food Services

Document:	Quality Manual	Reference:	QM
		Issue:	1.0
Title:	11 Customer-supplied	Date:	13-6-95
	Product	Page:	1 of 1

There are no items that are supplied by a customer and included in a product which is then sold back to the customer.

Should this become necessary, the appropriate procedure will be followed and documentation will be raised as required by CP 027 – Design and Development of New Products.

Originated by: **Authorized by:**

Date: **Date:**

QFS Quality Food Services

Document:	Quality Manual	Reference:	QM
		Issue:	1.0
Title:	12 Product Identification	Date:	13-6-95
	and Traceability	Page:	1 of 1

The company policy requires that record-keeping procedures are such that:

- Batch codes of received raw and packaging materials are recorded and can be related to their use in company products.
- All components of products, and the packaged products, will carry a company code which allows the product to be traced back to the date of production and the production line upon which it was made.
- Warehouse procedures will be such that the codes on delivered product can be related to delivery notes to customers.

Details can be found in the appropriate departmental procedures.

Originated by: **Authorized by:**

Date: **Date:**

QFS   Quality Food Services

Document:	Quality Manual	Reference:	QM
		Issue:	1.0
Title:	13 Inspection and	Date:	13-6-95
	Testing	Page:	1 of 1

1. Incoming goods

   Incoming raw and packaging materials will be received into the company according to procedure CP 028 – Receipt of Raw and Packaging Materials, and CP 004 – Sampling.

   Methods of analysis and laboratory calibration methods are specified in procedures CP 022 and CP 023.

2. In-process inspection and testing

   In-process inspection and testing will be carried out in accordance with the production manuals and quality procedures.

   The departmental manuals will specify authorities for dealing with nonconformances.

3. Final inspection and testing

   Quality assurance procedures ensure that at each stage of the process specifications are achieved, and process quality control (PQC) records demonstrate this.

   Responsibility for release of product to distribution rests with the end-of-line PQC operator, who applies the identification label to the pallet.

Originated by:	Authorized by:
Date:	Date:

QFS   *Quality Food Services*

Document:	Quality Manual	**Reference:**	QM
		Issue:	1.0
Title:	14 Inspection, Measuring	**Date:**	13-6-95
	and Test Equipment	**Page:**	1 of 1

All critical inspection, measuring and test equipment will be calibrated at specified intervals using specified methodology. Calibrated instrumentation and a detailed record of the calibration will be maintained for each instrument.

Calibration of inspection, measuring and test equipment in the plant will be specified in production manuals and quality procedures.

An inventory of instrumentation to be calibrated will be given in the production manual, together with details of target reading and tolerances required, and the standard against which the calibration is to be made.

Similarly, an inventory of laboratory equipment requiring calibration, together with calibration records will be maintained by the laboratory. Procedure CP 024 refers.

When an instrument fails its calibration, the implications for all product made since the last acceptable calibration will be reviewed by the Technical Manager and the Manufacturing Manager. A record of that review will be kept, including implementation of corrective action.

Originated by: **Authorized by:**

Date: **Date:**

QFS   Quality Food Services

Document:	Quality Manual	**Reference:**	QM
		Issue:	1.0
Title:	15 Inspection Measuring	**Date:**	13-6-95
	and Test Status	**Page:**	1 of 1

Any nonconforming items, be they raw or packaging materials, work-in-progress or finished product, will be labelled with the distinctive hold notices, signed and dated, bearing the reason for the nonconformity.

Management of nonconforming items will be carried out as specified in procedures CP 007 and CP 008.

Originated by: **Authorized by:**

Date: **Date:**

QFS   Quality Food Services

Document:	Quality Manual	Reference:	QM
		Issue:	1.0
Title:	16 Control of	Date:	13-6-95
	Nonconforming Items	Page:	1 of 1

Any nonconforming materials, work-in-progress or finished goods shall be isolated by responsible management using the distinctive hold notices.

The hold notices will bear the reasons for the nonconformity and will be signed and dated.

The Technical Manager will review the nonconformity with the Manufacturing Manager and determine corrective action.

Decisions will be made by the nominated authorities in accordance with procedures CP 007 and CP 008.

Originated by: **Authorized by:**

Date: **Date:**

QFS   Quality Food Services

Document:	Quality Manual	Reference:	QM
		Issue:	1.0
Title:	17 Corrective Action	Date:	13-6-95
		Page:	1 of 1

The company fosters the concept of corrective action and maintains procedures for control of nonconforming materials, work-in-progress and finished product.

The internal audit programme identifies nonconformances, and reviews and implements corrective action.

The Technical Manager has the responsibility for ensuring that decisions regarding nonconformity are fully implemented.

Also, the records of incidence of nonconformity will be considered by the General Manager at the half-yearly reviews.

Originated by: **Authorized by:**

Date: **Date:**

QFS   Quality Food Services

Document:	Quality Manual	**Reference:**	QM
		Issue:	1.0
Title:	18 Handling, Storage, Packaging,	**Date:**	13-6-95
	Preservation and Delivery	**Page:**	1 of 1

1. General

   There are established methods for the handling, storage, packaging, preservation and delivery of materials received into the company. These are covered in the warehouse manual.

   The packaging of products distributed by the company is specified in the production manuals.

2. Goods inwards

   The warehouse management is responsible for the receive and store function, deliveries from suppliers being booked into a schedule.The detailed operation is described in the departmental manual.

   Raw and packaging materials are taken to the receiving area, checked for quantity, punctuality and damage, entered into the warehouse computer, and stored in the appropriate area. Store location is also entered.

3. Final packing and palletization

   The details of final packing and palletization of finished products can be found in the appropriate packing specification and production manuals.

   The quantity of the finished product on the pallet will be part of the process quality control (PQC) checks, whereby an operator will inspect the pallet.

4. Despatch

   The quantity of material produced will be recorded by production. Records of despatch and material movements will be maintained by warehouse staff.

5. Storage

   Warehouse facilities are provided on site at third-party locations. Materials and products will be stored in the appropriate facilities, specified in the production manuals.

6. Delivery/distribution

   Instructions for stock movements are issued by the Distribution Department, who also control the type and conditions of transport.

Originated by: **Authorized by:**

Date: **Date:**

QFS   Quality Food Services

Document:	Quality Manual	Reference:	QM
		Issue:	1.0
Title:	19 Quality Management	Date:	13-6-95
		Page:	1 of 1

1. General

    This section summarizes the policy and procedures by which quality standards are set, controlled and audited in the factory.

2. Receipt and examination of incoming materials

    All materials are received as good, but are liable to random audit by the laboratory. The Vendor Assurance programme – procedures CP 013 and CP 014 – assures the reliability of suppliers.
    When inspection is necessary, procedures CP 004 – Sampling, and laboratory procedures CP 022, CP 023 and CP 024 are relevant.

3. Process quality control (PQC) procedures

    All manufacturing and packaging processes will be controlled by PQC checks to the targets and tolerances specified in the relevant production manuals, which will also define the methodology.
    PQC records will be signed by the production operator and stored in the Quality Department. PQC procedures and records will be audited by the Quality Department.

    Nonconforming product will be dealt with in accordance with procedure CP 008.

4. Final product assessment

    During each shift of production, finished product will be sampled from the end of each production line. Laboratory procedures will identify specific tests for each product type and records of all tests performed will be maintained. Procedures CP 023 and 024 refer.

5. Inspection and test equipment

    All equipment used to measure parameters that are critical to product quality, be they PQC controls or laboratory checks, shall be calibrated against the appropriate standard. This should be done at a frequency that ensures the equipment remains within calibration, or annually, whichever is the shorter. Calibration will be managed by the Quality Department, and records of these calibrations will be maintained in the appropriate department. Procedures CP 024 and 027 refer.

Originated by: **Authorized by:**

Date: **Date:**

QFS   Quality Food Services

Document:	Quality Manual	Reference:	QM
		Issue:	1.0
Title:	20 Laboratory	Date:	13-6-95
		Page:	1 of 1

1. General

   The function of the laboratory is:

   • to audit the quality of raw and packaging materials;
   • to manage the calibration of all necessary equipment;
   • to audit the hygiene procedures and state of housekeeping;
   • to maintain appropriate records.

2. Nonconforming materials or product

   All nonconforming materials and product identified in the company shall be isolated and managed in accordance with procedures CP 007 – Control of Nonconforming Materials – and CP 008 – Control of Nonconforming Product.

3. Inspection of measuring and test equipment

   All equipment used in the company to measure parameters associated with product quality shall be calibrated under the supervision of the laboratory.

   Procedures CP 024 and 027 refer.

4. Hygiene and housekeeping

   Hygiene and housekeeping audits will be carried out to ensure that correct cleaning procedures are being followed and that the required standards are being achieved.

   The audits shall be carried out in accordance with procedures defined in the Quality Department manual.

5. Methods of analysis

   All analyses shall be carried out according to CP 022 – Methods of Analysis.

Originated by: **Authorized by:**

Date: **Date:**

QFS   Quality Food Services

Document:	Quality Manual	Reference:	QM
		Issue:	1.0
Title:	21 Quality Records	Date:	13-6-95
		Page:	1 of 1

All quality records will be filed and stored by the Quality Department for a period of 5 years.

The PQC section of each production manual will specify which quality record should be kept.

Quality records include:

- minutes of General Manager's review;
- internal and external audit reports;
- minutes of supplier contact meetings;
- customer complaint reviews.

Originated by: **Authorized by:**

Date: **Date:**

QFS   Quality Food Services

Document:	Quality Manual	Reference:	QM
		Issue:	1.0
Title:	22 Internal Quality Audit	Date:	13-6-95
		Page:	1 of 1

The Technical Manager will maintain a schedule of internal audits of all procedures, departmental manuals and documents, at a minimum frequency of every 6 months. The objective is to ensure that all procedures are up to date and are being observed, and that specified records are being maintained.

A group of people drawn from all departments and all levels of the company structure will be trained for this purpose. No individuals will audit their own department and audit reports will be retained by the Technical Manager. Procedure CP 006 refers.

Originated by:	Authorized by:
Date:	Date:

QFS   Quality Food Services

Document:	Quality Manual	**Reference:**	QM
		Issue:	1.0
Title:	23 Training	**Date:**	13-6-95
		Page:	1 of 1

The policy of the company is to provide the following training:

1. Induction training

    Induction training is provided for all new employees during the early weeks of their employment. The objective is to ensure that all employees are integrated into the organization and become committed to the business. An awareness of the company is given together with knowledge of policies, products and structure. Emphasis is also given to safety, hygiene and quality management policies.

2. Job training

    Job training is given to help each employee reach maximum effectivenes as quickly as possible. In a Service Department an experienced employee will be assigned to give the necessary assistance and guidance. In Production Departments the group trainer will be responsible for on-the-job training.

3. Further training

    Further training is given to:

    • help individuals achieve performance improvements and widen their skills;
    • assist those suitable for promotion to take advantage of opportunities.

    The training needs are compiled into an annual training plan, which is regularly reviewed and updated by each manager.

4. Training records

    Records of all training undertaken are maintained to allow identification of each individual's capabilities and to monitor the effectiveness of training.

    Details of training are monitored by each department.

    Training records are stored in the Personnel Department for the duration of an individual's employment with the company.

Originated by:	**Authorized by:**
Date:	**Date:**

QFS   Quality Food Services

Document:	Quality Manual	Reference:	QM
		Issue:	1.0
Title:	24 Statistical Techniques	Date:	13-6-95
		Page:	1 of 1

The only regular application of statistical techniques is within the formal weight management programme to achieve the requirements of weights and measures legislation.

If use of statistical techniques becomes necessary, instructions will be issued by the Technical Department.

Originated by:	Authorized by:
Date:	Date:

QFS   Quality Food Services

Document:	Quality Manual	Reference:	QM
		Issue:	1.0
Title:	25 Index of Company	Date:	13-6-95
	Procedures	Page:	1 of 1

1. Document control
2. Procedures
3. Departmental manuals
4. Sampling
5. Contract packing
6. Internal auditing
7. Control of nonconforming materials
8. Control of nonconforming products
9. Order entry and processing
10. Generation, approval and issue of artwork
11. Planning procedures
12. Generation and placement of orders
13. Selection and approval of suppliers
14. Supplier performance
15. Training
16. Handling of complaints
17. Product recall
18. Crisis management
19. Coding policy
20. Auditing – finished product quality
21. Management information – quality performance
22. Laboratory procedures – methods of analysis
23. Laboratory procedures – test results
24. Laboratory procedures – calibration of equipment
25. Management of production trials
26. Calibration
27. Design and development of new products
28. Receipt of raw and packaging materials

Originated by:

Date:

Authorized by:

Date:

Appendix B

Accredited third-party certification bodies

This list of accredited certification bodies includes some who do not necessarily relate to the food industry.

Associated Offices Quality Certification Ltd (AOQC)
Longridge House, Longridge Place, Manchester M60 4DT, UK.
Tel. 0161 833 2295

ASTA Certification Services
23/24 Market Place, Rugby, Warks CV21 3DU, UK.
Tel. 01788 78435

BMT Quality Assessors Ltd (BMTQA)
Scottish Metropolitan Alpha Centre, Stirling University Innovation Park, Stirling FK9 4NF, UK.
Tel. 01786 50891

British Approvals Service for Cables (BASEC)
Silbury Court, 360 Silbury Boulevard, Milton Keynes MK9 2AF, UK.
Tel. 01908 691121

BSI Quality Assurance (BSIQA)
Business Development, PO Box 375, Milton Keynes MK14 6LL, UK.
Tel. 01908 220908

Bureau Veritas Quality International Ltd (BVQI)
70 Borough High Street, London SE1 1XF, UK.
Tel. 0171 378 8113

Central Certification Services (CCS)
Victoria House, 123 Midland Road, Wellingborough, Northants NN8 1LU, UK.
Tel. 01933 441796

Ceramic Industry Certification Scheme Ltd (CICS)
Queens Road, Penkull, Stoke on Trent ST4 7LQ, UK.
Tel. 01782 411008

Construction Quality Assurance (CQA)
Arcade Chambers, The Arcade, Market Place, Newark, Notts NG24 1UD, UK.
Tel. 01636 708700

Det Norske Veritas Quality Assurance Ltd (DNVQA)
Palace House, 3 Cathedral Street, London SE1 9DE, UK.
Tel. 0171 357 6080

Electrical Association Quality Assurance Ltd
30 Millbank, London SW1P 4RD, UK.
Tel. 0171 828 9227

Engineering Inspection Authorities Board (EIAB)
The Institution of Mechanical Engineers, 1 Birdcage Walk, London SW1H 9JJ, UK.
Tel. 0171 222 7899

Lloyds Register Quality Assurance Ltd (LRQA)
Hiramford, Middlemarch Office Village, Siskin Drive, Coventry CV3 4FJ, UK.
Tel. 01203 639566

National Approval Council for Security Systems (NACOSS)
Queensgate House, 14 Cookham Road, Maidenhead, Berks SL6 8AJ, UK.
Tel. 01628 37512

National Inspection Council Quality Assurance Ltd (NQA)
5 Cotswold Business Park, Millfield Lane, Caddington LU1 4AR, UK.
Tel. 01582 841144

SGS Yarsley International Certification Services Ltd
SGS House, Portland Road, East Grinstead, West Sussex RH19 4ET, UK.
Tel. 01342 410088

SIRA Certification Services
Saighton, Chester CH3 6EG, UK.
Tel. 01244 332200

Steel Construction QA Scheme Ltd (SCQAS)
4 Whitehall Court, Westminster, London SW1A 2ES, UK.
Tel. 0171 839 8566

The Loss Prevention Certification Board Ltd (LPCB)
Melrose Avenue, Borehamwood, Herts WD6 2BJ, UK.
Tel. 0181 207 2345

The Quality Scheme for Ready Mix Concrete (QSRMC)
3 High Street, Hampton, Middlesex TW12 2SQ, UK.
Tel. 01891 941 0273

TRADA Quality Assurance Services Ltd
Stocking Lane, Hughenden Valley, High Wycombe, Bucks HP14 4NR, UK.
Tel. 01240 245484

UK Certification Authority for Reinforcing Steels (CARES)
Oak House, Tubs Hill, Sevenoaks, Kent TN13 1BL, UK.
Tel. 01732 450000

Water Industry Certification Scheme (WICS)
Frankland Road, Blagrove, Swindon, Wilts SN5 8YF, UK.
Tel. 01793 410005

Appendix C

Guidance notes for the application of BS EN ISO 9001 : 1994 for the food and drink industry

Author: Sarah Davies
Market Sector Specialist
BSI Quality Assurance

These guidance notes have been prepared by a committee of representatives from food and drink organisations and certification bodies. Acknowledgement is made of the role of the co-operating organisations in drafting the document

Authorised

Martyn Reed:
Quality Manager, Business Development

Jeff Bulled:
Director, Business Development

TABLE OF CONTENTS

Appendix C

CO-OPERATING ORGANISATIONS
These guidance notes were prepared by a committee of representatives from the organisations listed below:

- British Quality Foundation – Food Sector
- BSI Quality Assurance
- Camden and Chorleywood Food Research Association
- Institute of Food Science and Technology
- Leatherhead Food Research Association
- Lloyds Register Quality Assurance Ltd

In addition, the following organisations were consulted and their comments have been incorporated in these guidelines.

- The Biscuit, Cake, Chocolate and Confectionery Alliance
- Brewers and Licensed Retailers Association
- Food and Drink Federation
- Dairy Industry Federation
- Maltsters Association of Great Britain

1. SCOPE AND FIELD OF APPLICATION AND INTRODUCTION

Scope and field of application

These guidance notes apply to parties involved in all aspects of the food and drink industry including sourcing, processing and packaging food and drink products.

The purpose of these guidance notes is to assist directors, managers and staff in applying the requirements of ISO 9001 and 9002 to the organisation during the development and implementation of a quality system.

These guidance notes should be read in conjunction with the standard and are not intended to replace or supersede any part of it.

The introductory sections of this document are intended to explain the background to the standard and highlight the main benefits of implementing a quality system. A more detailed explanation of each clause of the standard, as it applies to the food and drink industry, then follows.

What is the BS EN ISO 9000?

The standard is simply a specification for a quality system consisting of 20 clauses directed at the quality management process of the organisation. It provides a framework consisting of a range of processes, such as management review, training-needs analysis, and customer-needs evaluation, as well as requirements for continuous improvement and monitoring of the system. The standard is not prescriptive: it allows managers the freedom to implement methods that best suit the organisation's business needs. Managers should not try to mould the business operations around the requirements of the standard – quite the reverse – the requirements of the standard should be integrated into the operation. Where areas of the standard are not addressed, action should be taken to ensure the quality management system is complete.

NB: It should be recognised that those companies/businesses seeking certification can do so for individual parts of their operations. It is not essential to register the whole company at the initial assessment, providing the scope of certification is clearly defined (see definitions). Subsequent registrations can be added to the initial registration.

There are two versions of the standard applicable to the food and drink industry: BS EN ISO 9001 and BS EN ISO 9002 (henceforth referred to as ISO 9001 and ISO 9002). It is important to identify the correct version early in your implementation programme. The main differentiation between the two versions of the standard is the incorporation of design requirements (see 4.4) within ISO 9001. The certification body can assist in identifying the most applicable version by discussing with you the intended scope of certification. ISO 9001 is not necessarily more difficult or complex than ISO 9002 and may be more appropriate to your business.

A note on ISO 9001

Design control in the food and drink industry frequently relates to new product development but could also encompass process development. A company that develops new products for specific customers, e.g.: distributors' own brand products, is likely to choose to be assessed against the requirements of ISO 9001, if it wishes to include that activity in its scope of registration.

A note on maintenance of records

Certification bodies expect to see that a system has been established to store and maintain records. They will not necessarily expect to see the accumulated records of three years of operation (at the initial assessment), but they will expect sufficient records to be available to demonstrate the effective management of the quality system.

A note on Hazard Analysis and Critical Control Point (HACCP)

Within the food and drink industry, HACCP is a well-known technique used to analyse potential hazards in an operation, identifying where these may occur and deciding which are critical to consumer safety.

The hazards may be physical, chemical or microbiological and can occur during all stages of the manufacturing process – from raw materials through to consumption by the consumer. Appropriate action can be taken to ensure that areas identified as critical control points (CCPs) are kept under control and not allowed to endanger the items produced.

ISO 9000 provides an excellent foundation for many initiatives and HACCP fits particularly well into this model. It is worth bearing in mind that, as both ISO 9000 and HACCP are fundamental to the running of your business, they should not be treated separately. These techniques work best when linked together. HACCP is used to identify the CCPs, the ISO 9000 system is used for the control and monitoring of such points. Procedures for conducting a HACCP study can easily be documented within the quality system. The diagram below shows how ISO 9001 and HACCP compliment each other.

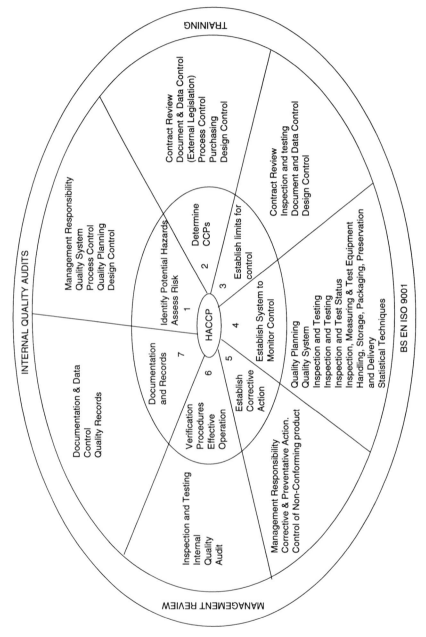

The links between BS EN ISO 9001 and HACCP

The diagram shows a wheel with concentric rings.

Outer ring labels: TRAINING, INTERNAL QUALITY AUDITS, MANAGEMENT REVIEW

Inner HACCP hub with numbered segments:

HACCP

1 — Identify Potential Hazards Assess Risk
2 — Determine CCPs
3 — Establish limits for control
4 — Establish System to Monitor Control
5 — Establish Corrective Action
6 — Verification Procedures Effective Operation
7 — Documentation and Records

Outer segment labels:

Management Responsibility
Quality System
Process Control
Quality Planning
Design Control

Contract Review
Document & Data Control (External Legislation)
Process Control
Purchasing
Design Control

Contract Review
Inspection and testing
Document and Data Control
Design Control

Quality Planning
Quality System
Inspection and Testing
Inspection and Testing
Inspection and Test Status
Inspection, Measuring & Test Equipment
Handling, Storage, Packaging, Preservation and Delivery
Statistical Techniques

Management Responsibility
Corrective & Preventative Action.
Control of Non-Conforming product

Inspection and Testing
Internal Quality Audit

Documentation & Data Control
Quality Records

Documentation and Records

BS EN ISO 9001

INTRODUCTION

What is UKAS accreditation?

"UKAS accreditation" is the recognition by the United Kingdom Accreditation Service (UKAS) (formerly NACCB) of a certification body's competence to conduct assessment and issue certificates within specified sectors of industry.

NB: In the United Kingdom, the authority to accredit certification bodies is granted to UKAS by the Department of Trade and Industry. The major European equivalent is the Dutch body, RvA (Raad voor Accreditatie).

Why use ISO 9000?

Any organisation wishing to meet customer needs and manage their business processes effectively can benefit from having a quality management system in place. The system should be applied where it is seen to be of benefit to customers and quality of service, rather than creating bureaucratic procedures and applying these slavishly.

The advantages of introducing a quality management system can include:

1. It facilitates and improves efficiency, which can make the organisation more cost-effective.
2. It improves consistency of service performance and consequently raises customer satisfaction levels.
3. It requires a review of the organisation's operations, which encourages best practice and cross-fertilization of ideas across the company.
4. It improves customer perception of the organisation's image, culture and performance by showing the organisation's commitment to quality.
5. It involves the whole work force and thus improves communication, morale and job satisfaction – staff understand what is expected of them and each other.
6. It provides a competitive advantage, which can increase marketing and sales opportunities.
7. It aids continuous improvement, gained through regular audits and subsequent corrective actions.

Frequently, organisations find that the essential elements of a quality management system already exist and it is simply a question of enhancing their documentation and controls. Ideally, the "system" should become integrated with the day-to-day running of the business, as quality becomes a way of life. There are some elements which stand alone, particularly management reviews and internal quality audits.

ASSESSMENT

The organisation should produce a quality manual. This is usually a high level document setting out the policy of the organisation to address each clause of the standard. The quality manual may be organized in the same order as the standard or in a manner more relevant to the business operation, with cross-references to the standard. As part of the assessment process, the certification body will normally want to review this document prior to conducting an assessment. This should provide an insight into the structure and activities of the organisation and their level of understanding of the standard.

At a mutually convenient time, the certification body will conduct an on-site assessment of the quality management system in operation. The duration of this assessment is dependent on the size and location(s) of the organisation. In the food and drink industry, this could typically range from a minimum duration of one day of assessment for a small organisation with a simple process at one location, two to eight days of assessment for a medium size organisation with larger, more complex processes on one location, up to very large, multi-site, complex organisations requiring more than 20 days. For medium to large organisations, an assessment team is normally used.

The initial assessment can be preceded by a pre-assessment, or trial/mock audit, which is designed to highlight any significant gaps in the quality management system or its implementation.

During the initial assessment, the assessors will want to observe the system in operation from the top down. They will be looking for all staff to have knowledge of their responsibilities towards quality within the organisation. Staff will not be expected to know the standard in any detail but will be expected to know their system and how it is applied.

Any problems identified during the assessment process are usually referred to as "nonconformities" and will be brought to the attention of the relevant managers as soon as possible. A nonconformity can be either "major" or "minor" in nature.

Major nonconformity

This relates to the absence, or total breakdown, of a system to meet the requirements of a clause of the standard. A number of minor nonconformities listed against one clause can represent total breakdown of a system and thus be considered a major nonconformity.

Minor nonconformity

This relates to either a failure to meet one requirement of a clause of the standard, or a single observed lapse in following one item of a company procedure.

If the assessors judge that, despite minor nonconformities, the system essentially meets the requirements of the standard, they will normally recommend certification, subject to the organisation submitting a corrective action plan setting out how the nonconformities will be dealt with. Once this has been accepted, the recommendation is then formally agreed by the certification body's executives and a certificate issued.

If the assessors feel that they cannot recommend certification, owing to major nonconformities, then a recommendation for a partial or full re-assessment will normally be made.

After assessment, the certification body carries out periodic checks on the organisation to ensure the quality management system continues to meet the requirements of the standard. These continuing assessments are normally pre-announced.

2. REFERENCES

To help you implement your system, you may find the following references useful:

Food and Drink – Good Manufacturing Practice: A Guide to its Responsible Management (IFST (UK) 3rd Edition; 1991 ISBN : 0905 367081)

- BN EN ISO 8402 : 1991   Quality management and quality assurance. Vocabulary.
- BS 4778 : Part 2 : 1991   Quality vocabulary. Quality concepts and related definitions.
- BS EN ISO 9001 : 1994   Quality systems. Model for quality assurance in design, development, production, installation and servicing.
- BS 5750 : Part 4 : 1994   Quality systems. Guide to the use of BS EN ISO 9001.
- BS ISO 10005 : 1995   Quality management and quality system elements: guidelines for quality plans.
- BS ISO 10013 : 1995   Guidelines for developing quality manuals.
- BS 7000 : Part 1 : 1989   Design management systems. Guide to managing product design.
- BS 7850 : Part 1 : 1992   Total quality management. Guide to management principles.
- BS 7850 : Part 1 : 1992   Total quality management. Guidelines for quality improvement.

- UK Department of Health Product Recall Procedure
- Food Safety Act 1990

British Standards can be ordered from:

BSI Standards
389 Chiswick High Road
London
W4 4AL
Tel: 0181 996 7000
Fax: 0181 996 7001

3. DEFINITIONS

In addition to the definitions given in BS EN ISO 8402, the following also apply:

Contract	Agreed requirements between a supplier and a customer, transmitted by any means.
Good Manufacturing Practice	The combination of manufacturing and quality procedures aimed at ensuring that products are consistently manufactured to their specifications. A full description of GMP is found in Food and Drink – Good Manufacturing Practice: A Guide to its Responsible Management – IFST (UK) 3rd Edition; 1991 : ISBN 0905 367081.
Hazard Risk Analysis	A method of analysing a process to clearly determine the inherent risks or hazards associated with it, in order to implement the most effective course of preventive action (for example, HACCP – Hazard Analysis and Critical Control Points).
Primary production	The production of foodstuffs that are supplied in a raw state.
Product (or Service)	The output that an organisation supplies to the purchaser.
Purchaser (or Customer)	The organisation purchasing the supplier's product.
Quality plan	A document setting out the specific quality practices, resources and sequence of activities relevant to a particular product, service, contract or project.
Scope of certification	A precise definition of the organisation's activities that are the subject of assessment for certification.
Secondary production and manufacture	Foodstuffs supplied that have undergone a manufacturing process that has altered the taste, colour or form of the primary production foodstuff.
Subcontractor	The organisation supplying a material or service to the supplier.
Supplier	The organisation seeking registration.
Tender	Offer made by a supplier in response to an invitation to supply goods or services.

4. THE STANDARD

This section of the guidance notes contains a more detailed explanation of each clause of the standard.

The twenty clauses of the standard are numbered 4.1 to 4.20 and this format has been used in numbering the following paragraphs. These should be read in conjunction with the corresponding clauses of the standard.

4.1 Management responsibility

4.1.1 Quality policy

There should be a documented quality policy, originated and endorsed in a meaningful manner by a relevant senior executive, and regularly reviewed. This clearly defined statement should set out the supplier's goals as they relate to the customer's expectations and needs.

There should be objective evidence to show that the policy statement has been implemented and understood at all levels within the organisation, e.g. placing policy statements on notice boards or quality briefings.

4.1.2 Organisation

4.1.2.1 Responsibility and authority

The quality system should clearly demonstrate the responsibilities and authorities of those who work within the system.

4.1.2.2 Resources

No industry specific guidance considered necessary. General guidance can be found in ISO 9004.

4.1.2.3 Management representative

Existing management should appoint a member of its own management team with clearly defined authority. Reporting should cover the continuing effectiveness of the system, and potential for improvement.

4.1.3 Management review

Management review should be carried out periodically to confirm that the whole system, including the quality policy, is effective. It is unlikely that the effectiveness of the system can be reviewed adequately if the period between reviews exceeds one year. These reviews should take into account, as a minimum, the results of internal quality audit, corrective and preventive action, the control of subcontractors and customer complaints, and other indicators of the effectiveness of the quality system.

4.2 Quality system

4.2.1 General

The quality system should ensure that all those activities within the organisation that could impact on the quality of the product are consistently defined (which usually means documented) and effectively implemented.

Above all, the structure of the quality system should be right for the company. This should address relevant codes of practice, and legislative requirements, e.g. weight control, hazard risk analysis, etc.

The standard requires the preparation of a quality manual which will clearly describe the structure of the quality system and act as a road map through it.

4.2.2 Quality system procedures

The company should recognise the balance to be made between documenting procedures and training and experience, and construct the procedures accordingly. The best rule of thumb is that detailed procedures or instructions will be required when the absence of them will adversely affect the level of product quality or service.

4.2.3 Quality planning

Quality activities should be systematically planned and defined, so the outcome of the activities complies with the specified requirements.

Quality plans that are specific to a company's products and processes can be prepared in a number of different ways, e.g. worksheets, flowcharts, business plans, hazard risk analysis and product specifications.

4.3 Contract review

In any situation there are tenders, contracts or orders between a supplier and a customer, contract review applies. This clause of the standard is key to establishing your customer's requirements, and most importantly, clarifying whether your company has the capability to meet those requirements. Customers' requirements will vary, from simple sales orders for standard products, call-offs against a pre-agreed annual contract, variable demands made against a sales forecast or requirements to produce technical product specifications and quality control inspection specifications. All customer requirements must be agreed between the customer and the supplier, and if the supplier cannot meet any or all of the stated requirements, the customer must be notified.

The methods used to demonstrate contract review will vary, but can include telephone messages, sales order information, signed tender documents or meeting minutes.

Compliance with current legislation is an inherent customer requirement. When exporting, consideration should be given to the relevant country's legislation.

4.4 Design control

4.4.1 Introduction

The terminology of this clause of the standard may be unfamiliar to many in the food industry. However, the processes involved are those that are commonly applied during product development. For example, the statement of customer requirements in a product development brief: the designation of development milestone meetings where development samples are assessed before approval is given to proceed to the next development stage; verification through challenge testing or shelf-life determination and validation through market research and transit tests.

The intention of this clause of the standard is to ensure that the specification of materials, processes, packaging, and product, arrived at through the development process meets the identified needs of the customer. There may be a great deal of creativity involved in such a process, in addition to technical expertise, and the design control system adopted can be contrived to give scope to creative flair.

In some circumstances modifications to a product may be of a trivial nature and the possibility of failing to meet customer requirements is negligible. In these instances the initiation of such a change may not require the full implementation of the design procedure. However, the criteria and authority for permitting minor modifications, and the methods of verification and validation should be clarified in the quality system. Procedures should be written to describe the way in which control and verification takes place during design so that product requirements are met.

157

4.4.2 Design and development planning

A plan should be prepared describing all development activity. Key points to include in any plan are the identification of those responsibilities for carrying out the development processes, ensuring they are able to carry out their responsibilities effectively and all key stages in the process. As the design (or new product, or new recipe) evolves, the plan will need to be updated.

4.4.3 Organisational and technical interfaces

Problems tend to occur at interfaces between different functional groups, usually due to communication difficulties and one group not realising that they are part of an internal 'customer-supplier' chain. Care should be taken to ensure that *all* members of the design process are clear as to their requirements, and that good communication reigns.

4.4.4 Design input

There are many design input requirements relating to a product. As a minimum these include statutory and regulatory requirements, and any which may derive from contract review, such as shelf life, compositional claims, style of packaging and price point. All of these input requirements must be accurately captured in the design process, and any which are conflicting or ambiguous should be resolved quickly with the relevant personnel.

4.4.5 Design output

The results of the development process (a new product, or new recipe, for example) should be measured against clear acceptance criteria (such as food safety and hygiene requirements, good manufacturing practice and other regulations). Verification and validation of the new product need to be included in the development plan. The chart below compares these activities, including design review.

Design control 'tool'	How to use	Further notes
Review	Where appropriate, to check progress of the design plan against key parameters.	Ensures that things are progressing as expected. May involve multi-disciplinary team, and will involve general records.
Verification	Ongoing process, which can include testing at stages in the process, or comparisons with known, proven, products.	Verification will check that any product claims can be substantiated, such as formal nutritional analysis, ingredients, etc.
Validation	At the end of the design process, to ensure that the new product meets user needs.	May be performed with specific target user groups (e.g. children's foods etc.) or by test marketing. Will check that all customer requirements can be met by the new product.

4.4.6 Design review

The frequency and composition of the team or particular individual performing the review would differ for each company and possibly each new design activity. The reviews should ensure that the design process stays relevant to input requirements and on target.

4.4.7 Design verification

Within the food and drink industry verification activities can include testing, tasting and reviews by selected user panels.

4.4.8 Design validation

The final validation of the product will confirm (or not) the acceptance of the product to the defined user group. In the food and drink industry this can include test marketing, trial production runs and invited consumer test panels.

4.4.9 Design changes

Any changes to the design after the processes detailed above have been successfully carried out must occur, as described within documented procedures, and the utmost care should be taken to ensure that changes will not adversely affect product safety, method of manufacture or legislative requirements.

4.5 Document and data control

4.5.1 General

Policy manuals, procedures and work instructions all form part of the documented system. Examples of other documentation utilised in the industry which are part of the system are:

- specifications, i.e. for raw materials, processing and products.
- drawings, e.g. artwork for packaging.
- current legislation and codes of practice.
- other externally generated documents, e.g. equipment manuals.

These should also be under document control.

4.5.2 Document and data approval and Issue

No industry specific guidance considered necessary. General guidance can be found in ISO 9004.

4.5.3 Document and data changes

No industry specific guidance considered necessary. General guidance can be found in ISO 9004.

4.6 Purchasing

4.6.1 General

General purchasing covers all materials and services used by the supplier to meet customer requirements. For example, the following may be included:

- ingredients
- processing aids
- processing water and water treatment
- maintenance, equipment, packaging and food contact
- sub-contract operations

- testing and laboratory services
- hygiene services and pest control
- transport
- warehousing (of both raw materials and finished products)
- distribution

The level of control a company wishes to exert over a supplier will depend on the nature and intended use of the material. Anything used as an ingredient, or coming into direct contact with the produce, will probably need tighter controls than, say, office equipment.

This will link into the determination of CCPs in a risk analysis programme.

4.6.2 Evaluation of subcontractors

Criteria for subcontractor acceptability should be established and records of compliance maintained. Consideration should be given to historical performance records and the risk of the material or service to your operation. This also applies to new subcontractors' material.

4.6.3 Purchasing data

Purchasing of raw materials or other primary products should be covered by some form of specification. Specifications should accommodate the inherent variability of such products and encompass the need for any special controls necessary to maintain their integrity, including the requirement to meet current legislation.

4.6.4 Verification of purchased products

4.6.4.1 Supplier verification at subcontractor's premises

This applies when a company verifies and releases raw materials at the supplier's premises.

4.6.4.2 Customer verification of subcontracted product

This applies when, as part of the contract with a customer, the company has agreed that the customer will have access to the company's sources of supply, e.g. raw materials, etc.

4.7 Control of customer supplied product

Customer supplied product is a raw material or packaging material supplied by the customer for processing with a particular product. It could also cover specific additional items to be incorporated into the finished product, such as a 'free gift' added into the final pack.

4.8 Product identification and traceability

It is a legal requirement in this industry that there is a system for batch or lot traceability (see The Food (Lot Marking) Regulations 1992). It is the responsibility of the supplier to determine what constitutes a batch or lot, other than where it is specifically part of the customer requirement. This will vary depending on the industry, and the potential risk of the product.

Where the customer requires the product to be identified by a specific mark or code, a system should be implemented for the verification of that mark or code.

Due heed should be given to identification of systems which are necessary to comply with any legal requirements or codes of practice such as that of the UK Department of Health product recall procedure (or national equivalent).

Consideration should also be given to including plans for product recall, including definition of responsibilities.

4.9 Process control

The following headings highlight certain aspects whose relevance should be considered at all stages from raw materials reception to product delivery, however, this is neither exhaustive nor prescriptive.

- Environment

  Atmosphere, soil, ground water and invasive life forms from microbes to mammals.

- Buildings

  All buildings including facilities for storage, manufacture, personal hygiene, packing, handling, testing and despatch, as well as administration offices in the proximity should be considered.

- Plant equipment and utilities

  This includes hygienic design of plant and equipment as well as the cleaning processes required. Equipment should have suitable maintenance to ensure it remains capable of processing to the specified standards.

- Personnel

  This includes provision of appropriate workwear (coats, boots, hats etc) and training in appropriate hygienic practices.

- Legislation

  The requirements of relevant legislation applicable to personal hygiene, and protective clothing to be used.

- Health screening

  Evidence of screening procedures (where legally or otherwise specified) and their maintenance for food handlers with respect to product safety.

- Criteria for workmanship

  Staff should be adequately trained and provided with the relevant work instruction/ standards/specifications/legislation (or any other suitable means).

- Cross contamination

  The risks arising from cross-contamination should be considered and systems installed to reduce this risk. (Hazard risk analysis can be part of this system.) This should be considered for raw materials, packaging and product.

- Computer failure

- Special processes

These are processes where the results cannot be fully verified by subsequent inspection and testing of the product. With adequate hazard risk analysis and effective controls it is likely that this area will be adequately covered. Examples are pasteurisation (milk), sterilisation (canning) and CIP (cleaning in place). As inspection and testing technology develops, techniques become available to verify some of these processes within acceptable timescales and without requiring destructive testing. However, it is still industry practice to validate these processes before general use in manufacturing.

4.10 Inspection and testing

The quality plan should identify key control points for raw materials, packaging, in-process and finished product testing. The mechanism for release of material should be defined. Hazard risk analysis could be used to identify key control points.

Tests based on senses

Tests that are based on sight, odour, taste and texture should combine the following elements:

- the holding of standard reference batches, where appropriate
- qualification, training and re-evaluation of testing personnel
- procedures to ensure long-term consistency.

Special tests

In-house tests that have been developed by modifying standard test methods or developed internally should be documented and validated.

Records of all inspection and tests should be maintained.

4.11 Controls of inspection, measuring and test equipment

The supplier should select and identify all pieces of equipment that are to be used to check conformity to specifications.

Selection

When selecting inspection, measuring and test equipment the following should be taken into consideration:

- does it provide acceptable measurements as required by the specification?
- what deviation from the normal value can be accepted over a period of time without detriment to product quality?
- is the piece of equipment sufficiently accurate for the measurements required?

Identification

Any piece of equipment used to check conformity to the specification should have its calibration status clearly identified. This may be a mark, an approved record, or any other method, but should be clear.

When a piece of equipment has been selected as being for comparative purposes (or 'indication') only, this too should be clear to the user. The system should ensure that the piece of equipment is not inadvertently used for critical measurements.

Calibration programme

Procedures should address the following:

- calibration schedule
- acceptance criteria
- check method
- where no national standards exist, the basis for calibrating equipment should be defined.
- where a piece of equipment is found to be out of calibration the validity of previous test results should be addressed. Consideration should be given to products produced since the last correct calibration result.
- a competent person should carry out the calibration.

Records should be maintained of calibration including certificates which are traceable to national standards (where applicable). Calibration certificates should also indicate measurement accuracy of equipment at the time of calibration (the "as found" reading).

4.12 Inspection and test status

There should be a clearly defined method for identification of inspection and test status to prevent inadvertent use.

This may mean pass/fail, acceptable/non-acceptable, awaiting inspection notices which clearly mark particular products, or any of a number of methods suitable for other applications.

4.13 Control of nonconforming product

Nonconforming products can be identified by inspection, customer complaint or internal quality audits, although it is always better for you to find the problem before your customer does. Systems should prevent inadvertent use of such products until a decision has been made as to how to deal with them. There are four possibilities for disposition of nonconforming product:

- it is reworked and reinspected to check conformity to specification
- an agreement is made with the customer for a concession
- the product is to be safely disposed of in accordance with any relevant regulations and guidance
- regrading for alternative use.

4.14 Corrective and preventive action

4.14.1 General

Systems should be in place both to ensure and record corrective action when things go wrong, and to prevent recurrence.

4.14.2 Corrective action

Where a problem has been identified, there is a need not only to correct the immediate situation but also to identify, where possible, the underlying cause. Once this has been identified, action should be taken to prevent recurrence. Corrective action should also be addressed in other areas, e.g. hygiene audits, pest control reports. Nonconforming service, e.g. late deliveries, should also be addressed.

4.14.3 Preventive action

Where appropriate, the use of hazard risk analysis techniques should be applied in fulfilling the preventative aspects of the standard (see also 4.2).

In order to improve the system, it is important that information derived from preventive action is fed back to management review.

4.15 Handling, storage, packaging, preservation and delivery

The supplier should ensure that product and materials are handled, stored, packed and preserved, and delivered under the right conditions to maintain the specified quality.

Factors which may be considered include:

- contract packaging
- control of specified artwork for packaging materials
- storage temperatures
- stock rotation
- shelf life
- delivery temperatures
- legislative requirements
- contamination risks
- environment and fabric of buildings
- hygiene and infestation control.

NB 'Preservation' does not refer to the addition of preservatives into a food or drink product.

4.16 Control of quality records

Quality records are those which demonstrate the effective management of the system and should therefore be retained.

Retention periods of all quality system records (e.g. purchasing, process control, contract review and records held as electronic data) should be specified and reflect both statutory regulations and product shelf-life.

System management records (e.g. internal audit, management review, system changes) retained for less than 3 years may be insufficient to demonstrate effectiveness.

4.17 Internal quality audits

A pre-planned schedule of internal audits should be compiled, ensuring that the whole system is covered over a stated timescale. This also includes remote locations. Audits, as a minimum, should check that:

- procedures are in place and are used correctly.
- procedures adequately describe the systems activities.
- procedures are effective.

They are of immense importance to a company, as they are the means of carrying out the 'self-check' on the health of the company, and performed well will give invaluable information to improve the business. Audits can also identify best practice situations, and may be extended to cover other areas, such as hygiene or housekeeping.

Appropriate records of audits should be maintained and audit summaries are normally presented as part of management review.

4.18 Training

A system for the identification and implementation of training needs should be in place for all staff.

Training records should be available for all members of staff within the quality system and these should include all types of training, i.e. in-house, on-the-job and external.

Training should include process activities, quality related functions and hygiene requirements.

4.19 Servicing

There are very few examples of contractually agreed servicing in the food and drink industry. However, examples are:

• Vending machines
• Refrigeration equipment supplied by ice cream manufacturers.

4.20 Statistical techniques

4.20.1 Identification of need

It is likely that companies in the food and drink industry will use statistical techniques in some form. They can be an effective method of evaluating the level of quality capability of any given process.

Statistical techniques relate to the use of sample measures of performance that are considered to be mathematically representative of a given situation or process. They are especially applicable in the establishment of process capability, on-line sampling, quality control analysis and statistical process control. Clause 4.9.(d) of the standard requires the use of "suitable process parameters" and, read in conjunction with this clause, it implies the use of appropriate statistical techniques.

4.20.2 Procedures

Having identified the relevant techniques, procedures should be written to describe the implementation and control of their application. These procedures may be most effective when written as an integral part of the process control procedures.

Appendix D

Guidance notes for the application of ISO 9002/EN 29002/BS 5750: Part 2 To the hotel and catering industry

BSI Quality Assurance

Page 1 QGN/66/392: Issue 1

FOREWORD

These guidelines have been prepared by a committee of representatives from hotel and catering organisations. Acknowledgement is made of the role of the co-operating organisations in drafting this document.

BSI Quality Assurance

British Hotels, Restaurants and Caterers Association

Campden Food and Drink Research Association

Department of Health

European Catering Association

Hotel, Catering and Institutional Management Association

Hotel and Catering Training Company

Leatherhead Food R.A.

The Mobile and Outside Caterers Association

1. INTRODUCTION

These notes are intended to provide guidance for the application of ISO 9002/EN 29002/BS 5750 Part 2 to the catering industry.

The guidance notes should be read in conjunction with the Standard, they are not intended to replace or supersede the Standard.

Additional guidance to the Standard is provided in ISO 9004/EN 29004/BS 5750: Part 0: Section 0.2 and ISO 9004-2/BS 5750 : Part 8.

The sections in these guidelines are numbered to correspond with the relevant section of the Standard.

The guidelines do not repeat the standard, but deal with those areas which are thought to need more explanation and clarification when implementing a quality system.

The guidelines are intended for caterers and businesses providing accommodation including leisure and/or food and beverage services. Businesses with leisure facilities should also refer to the Leisure Industry Guidelines.

2. REFERENCES

BS 5750 : Part 0 : Section 0.1 : 1987 Guide to Selection and Use.

BS 5750 : Part 0 : Section 0.2 : 1987 Guide to Quality Management and Quality Systems Elements.

BS 5750 : Part 2 : 1987 Quality System Specification for Production and Installation.

BS 5750 : Part 4 : 1990 Quality Systems Guide to the use of BS 5750.

BS 5750 : Part 8 : 1991 Guidelines for services.

BS 4778 – Quality Vocabulary.

Guidance notes on the application of ISO 9002/EN 29002/BS 5750 part 2 to the Leisure Industry.

3. DEFINITIONS

In addition to the definitions of BS 4778 : Part 1 – 1987, the following definitions apply:

Product/Service   The meal, facility or function provided by the supplier.

Purchase   The organisation or individual purchasing the hotel and/or catering service.

Standard   ISO 9002/EN 29002/BS 5750 : Part 2

Sub-contractor   The organisation supplying a material or service to the supplier.

Supplier   The organisation or individual providing the hotel and/or catering service.

4. QUALITY SYSTEM GUIDELINES

The sub-clause numbers in this clause directly relate to the sub-clause numbers of the standard.

4.1 Management Responsibility

4.1.1 Quality Policy

As stated in the note to clause 3.1 of BS 5750 : Part 0 : Section 0.1 *The quality policy forms one element of the corporate policy and is authorised by top management.* It should be signed by the Chief Executive or another senior manager with overall responsibility for quality. Consideration should be given to the inclusion of health and hygiene and customer service.

4.1.2 Organisation

4.1.2.1 Responsibility and Authority

The requirement is largely self-explanatory. There should be an organisation chart and defined responsibilities for those activities shown in that chart. This may be fulfilled by statements in the documented quality system or by references in the quality system to job descriptions.

Personnel identified should include all management as well as those with direct responsibility for quality within the organisation.

4.1.2.2 Verification Resources and Personnel

The specific requirements for inspection, test and monitoring of raw materials, in process and finished goods and the auditing of the quality system should be identified throughout the organisation and carried out by suitably qualified and trained personnel.

4.1.2.3 Management Representative

The management representative should have the organisational freedom and authority as described in clause 4.1.2.1. The management representative in some larger organisations might be referred to as the quality assurance manager. The management representative may have other jobs; the freedom referred to above only applies when he/she is acting in his/her quality assurance capacity.

4.1.3 Management Review

Management reviews should be undertaken at least once a year, under the direct control of senior management. Records of management reviews should be available, and indicate the actions decided upon, and the effectiveness of such actions should be considered during subsequent reviews. Records may be in the form of meeting minutes, and management reviews may form part of another meeting.

The agenda for this activity may include review of:

- internal quality audits
- customer complaints
- non-conforming materials
- sub-contractor performance
- training plan
- quality system improvements

The frequency of management reviews should be defined.

4.2 Quality System

The requirement for a 'documented quality system' means that a fully comprehensive written description of the company's system should be prepared covering all aspects of the standard. It should be borne in mind when drafting procedures, etc., that they could be used as the basis for external and internal audits.

When documenting a quality system, the skills and training of the staff need to be taken into account.

The format of the quality system documentation is not specified (guidance is given in clause 4.2 of BS 5750 : Part 4) but it should be designed specifically to meet company requirements.

4.3 Contract Review

Contract review should include the following:

- is the purchase requirement clearly specified?
- does the supplier have the capability to meet this requirement?

This clause of the standard applies to all levels of contact with the purchaser, not just formal written contracts. Examples of this could be:

- request for accommodation
- request for food or beverage
- booking of a conference facility

4.4 Document Control

Policy manuals, procedures and work instructions all form part of the document control system. Examples of other documentation utilised in the industry which should be under document control are as follows:

- approved suppliers list
- codes of practice
- current legislation
- dish specifications
- raw material specification

4.5 Purchasing

4.5.1 General

Purchasing covers all materials and services used by the supplier that can affect the quality of the product. For example, the following may be included:

- delivery services
- employment agencies
- hygiene services
- laundry supplies
- pest control
- raw materials

4.5.2 Assessment of Sub-Contractors

The criteria for sub-contractor acceptability should be established and records of compliance maintained. Where this is not possible (for example, in cases where goods are purchased in local wholesalers or retailers), responsibility for purchasing should be defined.

4.5.3 Purchasing Data

Where raw materials specifications exist, they should be referenced on relevant purchasing documentation. This may not be practical for all materials purchased (for example, canned goods may be purchased against the suppliers standard product list). However, references to all materials on purchase orders should be clear and concise.

4.5.4 Verification of Purchased Products

No further guidance is considered necessary.

4.6 Purchaser Supplied Product

For the caterer, *purchaser supplied product* could be kitchen facilities and the quality system should include procedures to ensure correct usage and maintenance of these facilities. A system should also exist for dealing with damages or the problems related to these.

For hotels, *purchaser supplied product* could be wines, flowers, wedding cakes or equipment for use during a function.

4.7 Product Identification and Traceability

The degree of product identification and traceability should take into account whether the source of non-conformity can be readily identified. Traceability should also be considered in relation to staff involved in the provision of the service.

Suppliers providing food and drink should consider traceability from receipt through to purchaser.

4.8 Process Control

Process control covers all activities, i.e. food production and service procedures to enable the supplier to meet requirements.

The following should be considered under process control:

- areas of responsibility, including work instructions. (Work instructions need only be issued where their absence would adversely affect the quality of the service or product – a balance should be found between experience, training and work instructions.)
- hygiene in relation to product, including food handling and condition of facilities to be used
- legislation and codes of practice
- risks arising from cross contamination
- identification and disposal of waste products
- customer care system (including *good housekeeping*)
- maintenance of environmental systems

4.9 Inspection and Test

Criteria for acceptability of raw materials should be established and responsibility defined for the release of these materials. This should also be applied to in-process inspection (storage and cooking), and final inspection.

Records of all inspections and tests should be maintained.

Examples of relevant inspections are as follows:

- inspection of bedrooms
- kitchen hygiene
- service standards by personnel performance

4.10 Inspection, Measuring and Test Equipment

Catering Industry

The fact that most equipment may be customer-owned does not negate the requirements for calibration of inspection and test equipment.

Hotel and Catering Industry

Consideration should be given to the inspection, measuring and test equipment that could affect the final quality of the product. In this industry it is mainly temperature measuring equipment which is critical. All calibration should be traceable to National Standards (where applicable). In the case of equipment used for indication purposes only (for example, oven temperatures), formal calibrating may not be necessary; but a programme for ensuring equipment performance should be in place.

Calibration should also be considered for:

- measurement of customer satisfaction
- optics in a bar

4.11 Inspection and Test Status

No further guidance is considered necessary.

4.12 Control of Non-Conforming Product

Non-conforming products or services may be identified by quality control inspections, customer complaints, or internal quality audits. Once identified, there should be a system of identification and possible segregation to prevent the product being inadvertently used or to prevent the non-conforming service being continued.

A decision should be made by a nominated representative, in respect of products, to:

- dispose of product safely
- regrade for alternative use
- use with concession from the customer

and in respect of services, to:

- reallocate duty
- retrain

4.13 Corrective Action

When a non-conformity has been identified, then the following actions may be instigated:

- analysis of processes within the system
- investigation of why the non-conformity has occurred
- agreement of preventative measures and timescales for action to be taken
- follow up action to ensure preventative measures have been implemented

4.14 Handling, Storage, Packaging and Delivery

The requirement is to ensure that the quality of the product is maintained throughout the process. Areas addressed should include the following (under the sub-headings given in the standard):

Handling

Correct handling of food by staff.

Packaging

Containers and food contact material – suitability for use and prevention of taint and cross contamination.

All legislative requirements (for example, contact packaging and temperature controls).

Storage

Temperature control, and the prevention of cross-contamination during storage.

Delivery

Temperature control of any delivery vehicles or special delivery containers used.

This clause also addresses the handling and delivery of the service, for example:

- counter service
- reception
- the delivery of the ordered product to the purchaser

4.15 Quality Records

Retention periods of all quality records (e.g. purchasing, process control, contract review etc) should be specified and reflect both statutory regulations and product shelf-life.

Records to demonstrate the effective management of the system should be retained.

System management records (e.g. internal audit, management review, system changes) retained for less than 3 years may not be sufficient to demonstrate effectiveness.

Certification bodies expect to see that a system has been established to store and maintain records. They will not necessarily expect to see the accumulated records of three years of operation (at the initial assessment), but they will expect sufficient records to be available to demonstrate the effective management of the quality system.

4.16 Internal Quality Audits

A pre-planned schedule of internal audits should be compiled to ensure checks are made on all aspects of the system. Audits should check to see if:

- the procedures are in place and are used correctly
- the procedures adequately describe the systems activities
- training is adequate

Records of audits should be maintained and a summary of audit findings presented at management review meetings.

Auditors should be trained and independent of the departments they are auditing.

4.17 Training

Records of training should be held for every member of staff, including internal, on-the-job and external training. A programme for the identification of training needs should be implemented taking into consideration legislative requirements.

The training needs of temporary staff should be considered.

4.18 Statistical Techniques

If these techniques are applied then procedures should be documented and records maintained.

Appendix E

New Zealand Q-Base code: quality management systems for small and medium-sized enterprises – general requirements TB 004 : 1995

Published with permission of
Q-Base New Zealand (A division of Telarc New Zealand)
Private Bag 28 901, Remuera, Auckland 1136, New Zealand

Table of Contents

0 Foreword

Why Q-Base?
Companies throughout the World are implementing ISO 9000 based quality management systems. By mid 1994 there were over 70,000 ISO 9000 certified companies in 76 countries. New certifications were being awarded at a rate of about 2700 per month.

178

In parallel with this explosive growth in ISO 9000 certification there has been a growing Worldwide concern about the applicability of the ISO 9000 series standards to small and medium sized enterprises.

The ISO 9000 standards have their origins in defence, aerospace and nuclear industry contractor control specifications of the 1950s and 1960s. The target audience for these precursor documents was the large business sector – the primary contractors. Their authors never envisaged that they should be applied to small businesses.

In most countries small businesses employing less than about ten people usually account for at least 80% of all business enterprises. If the threshold is raised to 20 employees this usually accounts for over 90% of businesses. It is questionable whether these small and medium sized enterprises should be required to implement the formal management systems and procedures, the organisational structures, and the documentation regimes required of larger organisations by the ISO 9000 standards.

Small businesses pushed by commercial pressures into the implementation of ISO 9000 systems face disproportionate problems compared to larger companies. The financial impact of the ISO 9000 certification is proportionally much greater for small businesses. The cost, time and effort of ISO 9000 implementation and certification do not increase linearly with company size. There are certain base costs that must be borne by every business, irrespective of its size. Larger companies also benefit from the inevitable economies of scale. One study suggests that it costs a 10 person company as much as five times more, per employee, to implement and certify an ISO 9000 quality system, than it costs a 100 person company.

Resources
Small companies rarely employ quality management professionals on their staff. This implies that they are much more likely to need the services (and consequent expense) of consultants to assist with their quality system development. At the same time they are also less well equipped to select knowledgeable consultants and to control and monitor their work to ensure that the quality systems they recommend are fit for purpose.

Small businesses are often chronically under-resourced. Owner–managers typically spend all day running the business then go home to catch up with the accounts and the other paperwork. Finding the time to plan and document a formal quality management system is difficult without taking on additional staff. But many small businesses are working on such low margins that an extra person is not a viable option.

The concept of documenting formal systems and procedures in a manual is often quite alien to small business operators. Many small businesses have grown out of the personal skills of their entrepreneurial owners. Practical, hands-on people prefer to get on with the job rather than write a manual about how to do it.

History

Telarc is New Zealand's leading quality system certification body, active in the field since 1984. Having encountered many small businesses struggling with ISO 9000 implementation – most under some commercial pressure to do so – it was realised that an alternative to ISO 9000 was required for these companies. After appropriate market research a special certification scheme to meet the needs of small businesses and their customers was developed. This scheme is known as the **Q-Base Programme**. The symbolism in the name indicates that it is a basic, entry level programme; a base that can be built upon to full ISO 9000 compliance, at a later date, if required.

Q-Base takes the requirement of the ISO 9000 standards (pitched about halfway between ISO 9002 and ISO 9003) and presents them free of jargon, suitable for use by small and medium sized enterprises that do not employ quality management professionals. The objective has been to identify the basic quality management disciplines that a small business must apply in order to give its customers confidence in the quality of its goods and services and in order to achieve the cost savings that come from effective quality systems.

1 Introduction

This code of quality management practice has been developed to provide small businesses with a model for their quality systems. It is based upon the ISO 9000 series of international quality system standards but recognises the less formal structures and systems required by small businesses.

The Q-Base Code will typically be adopted by small businesses:

- Wishing to demonstrate a formal commitment to customer satisfaction through quality management.
- Subcontracting to, or supplying companies that have ISO 9000 certification.
- Subcontracting to, or supplying government agencies, local authorities, public utilities and wholesale and retail traders.
- Wanting an entry level quality system that can be enhanced to full ISO 9000 compliance at a later date.

2 Q-Base Code

2.1 Management of the Quality System

Requirement

The company must appoint one of its staff to have overall responsibility for quality assurance in the day to day work of the organisation.

This must be a senior person with sufficient respect and authority in the company to be able to ensure that all other staff follow the quality assurance programme at all times.

The responsibility and authority of this Quality Co-ordinator must be defined in a written job description or similar document.

The chief executive of the company must review and sign this document to give it official backing and to demonstrate commitment to the quality assurance programme.

Guidance

In a small company the Chief Executive or Owner/Manager will usually be the Quality Co-ordinator. In a larger company the Quality Co-ordinator may be a department or branch manager.

If a consultant is employed to act as the Quality Co-ordinator the consultant's contract should endorse that he/she has sufficient authority to control the effectiveness of the quality system.

2.2 Control of Critical Documents and Records

Requirement

The company must have a system for uniquely identifying and controlling all its critical documents to ensure that only the current editions are in use and that no unauthorised changes are made.

The document control system must also ensure that copies of documents are given to everyone who needs them so that they are not tempted to rely on memory for critical information.

Quality records must be sufficient to demonstrate that all essential processes have been carried out and that all essential inspections or tests have been undertaken.

Quality records must be retained for an appropriate period. This period will depend upon the nature of the product or service and the length of time that it will be in use in the marketplace and during which quality problems are likely to come to light.

Guidance

Critical documents are those that are essential for ensuring the quality of products and services and the proper operation of the company's quality management system. They include drawings, material specifications, work instructions, customer orders and specifications, operation manuals, reference manuals, procedure manuals, job descriptions, regulations, etc.

The term "document" includes any method of recording or displaying information. Documents may be in the form of paper, computer disks, wall charts, posters, videos, photographs, etc. Whatever their format they should be controlled and authorised if critical to quality.

Records are an essential feature of any quality assurance system but they need not be extensive or exhaustive.

The key records necessary to demonstrate the performance of the quality assurance system should be listed. To ensure the system is easily checked, the records should show who is responsible for them, where they are kept and for how long.

2.3 Customer Needs

Requirement

The company must document and review all contracts (including verbal agreements) to supply customers with goods or services to ensure that:
(i) The customer's requirements are understood, and
(ii) The company has the capability to meet the customer's requirements.

Any amendments to a contract must be recorded and must be communicated to and agreed to by all interested parties.

Guidance

A contract is defined as any written or verbal agreement between the company and its customers and suppliers (communicated by any means) that commits the company to supply or purchase goods or services.

A major source of quality problems is a lack of effective communication between customers and suppliers.

Before accepting an order the company should ensure that it has the capability to meet the specified requirements. This might include having the trained staff, materials, production facilities, stock and all other resources necessary to complete the order on time and to the specification required.

Procedures should contain a process for customers to correctly authorise any agreed amendment in a customer's order.

2.4 Purchasing

Requirements

The company must have a system for controlling the materials, components and subcontract services that it buys.

Suppliers and subcontractors must be selected on the basis of the quality of their products or work and not on price alone.

A register of approved suppliers and subcontractors must be kept with information as to why they were selected as approved suppliers and how they are performing.

The company must also have procedures for checking that their suppliers deliver what was ordered, in the correct quantity, to the correct specification.

Guidance

The company should identify the critical materials and services that it buys. These are the items that must be correct if they are not to detract from the quality of its own goods or services.

Critical materials and services should only be purchased from approved suppliers or subcontractors.

2.5 Training and Work Instructions

Requirements

The company must ensure that its staff is fully trained for the work that it does. Where necessary, members of staff must be provided with written work instructions setting out how the company requires critical jobs or tasks to be carried out.

Records of training must be kept and staff competence must be regularly reviewed to determine whether retraining is required.

Guidance

A properly designed training programme will ensure that each person's training needs have been evaluated, and that appropriate training has been carried out by qualified people.

Training should be carried out by experienced staff with the proviso that they have been trained and competency rated as effective i.e. "trained trainers".

Training should always refer back to approved work instructions so that variations and inconsistencies are eliminated in the process.

Competency of staff may vary over time depending upon the complexity and nature of the tasks regularly undertaken.

A commitment to staff training is often a powerful indication of the company's overall commitment to quality.

Work processes should be studied to determine whether staff need ready access to work instructions. For most operations these will not be necessary but for some they are critical.

2.6 Inspection and Control of Substandard Work

Requirement

The company must draw up plans for the inspection of raw materials, components, work in progress and finished products.

The company must ensure that all measuring, test and inspection equipment used to verify or ensure product or service quality is calibrated, verified or checked to an accuracy appropriate for its use. This includes jigs, patterns, gauges, and other production aids.

All measurements made during inspections and tests must be evaluated, in terms of the accuracy of measurements required and the inherent capabilities of the equipment used, to determine the instrument's calibration requirements.

All calibrations must be traceable to the national standards of measurement.

The inspection status of materials and products, as they flow through the production process, must be clearly identified to indicate whether they have been inspected and are suitable for further processing; they have been inspected and have been found to be substandard or they are waiting inspection.

Once substandard materials or products have been detected the company must have formal procedures for disposing of them. They may be scrapped or re-worked. They may be sold as seconds or offered to the customers at a discount.

Whatever decision is made it must be made in a controlled manner by someone with specific authority for such decisions, and it must be recorded.

Guidance

Inspection Plans

Inspection plans should include (as appropriate):
• how the inspections are to be performed,
• what equipment is to be used,
• who is to carry out the inspections,
• how often,
• how many samples are to be checked,
• how samples are to be selected,
• the pass/fail criteria, and
• the type of inspection records that are to be kept.

Equipment Calibration

Common sense must be used in deciding on calibration requirements. If a micrometer is used to measure to the nearest millimetre then it may not need calibration, but if it is used to measure to 0.05 mm then regular calibration is essential. Calibration involves the comparison of a measuring instrument with another (reference) instrument of a higher order of accuracy. It is usual to work to an accuracy ratio of 10. Verification involves ensuring that an instrument is working to specifications. Checking of an instrument usually implies a low level comparison with a similar device. If two devices read the same, this provides a simple check that no gross errors have been introduced.

Inspection Status

Identification of inspection status may be achieved in a number of ways. Labels or tags may be used or special containers or special locations on the shop floor may be used for various materials in the three status categories.

Control of Substandard Work

The authority to make decisions about the treatment of substandard product should be defined and documented. All such decisions should be recorded and reviewed as part of the Quality Co-ordinator's system reviews.

2.7 Quality Improvements

Requirements

The company must have a procedure for investigating any incidence of substandard product, customer complaints and other quality failures to determine the root cause of the problems.

Corrective action must then be taken to ensure that a similar problem will not occur again. The effectiveness of the corrective action must be evaluated to ensure that it has rectified the root cause of the problem.

Guidance

The company should develop a formal Quality Improvement programme which analyses each problem, as it occurs, and attempts to find a permanent solution to prevent the same problem from happening again. This involves looking beyond the symptoms of the problem to find out why it happened in the first place.

Appendix F

Glossary

Assessors/assessment house A company or organization accredited by the responsible government department – in the UK it is the United Kingdom Accreditation Service (UKAS) – to assess candidate companies for certification to the standard.

BS 5750 The original British Standard for Quality Management Systems, which subsequently also became EN 29000 in Europe and ISO 9000 in the world. All three documents have now been amalgamated into one document – **BS EN ISO 9001 Series Standard for Quality Management Systems.**

Calibration The process of verifying that instruments used for measurement, as distinct from indications, are accurate to the national standard for the parameter concerned.

CEN, Comité Européen pour Normalisation European Standards Organization

Company quality manual The document laying out the principles by which an organization will achieve the requirements of BS EN ISO 9001.

Company quality policy The document issued by a Chief Executive defining the quality management objectives for the business concerned.

Corrective action Action taken to rectify a nonconformance.

COSHH regulations Control of Substances Hazardous to Health Regulations 1988.

Customer-supplied product Material or part product supplied by a customer to have value added, and then sold back to the customer.

Design management The procedure by which the design process is managed.

Document Controller The employee responsible for the issue, distribution and withdrawal of all documents associated with a quality management system.

Document review The activity in which assessors review system documentation to ensure that all clauses of the standard have been covered, before they progress to the full assessment.

Due Diligence defence A defence in English law, whereby a defendant can be found not guilty if it can be shown that 'all due diligence had been exercised, and all reasonable precautions taken, to ensure the offence would not occur'.

EN 29000 The European equivalent of BS 5750: they are identical.

Final assessment The act of assessment by assessors to determine whether the requirements of the standard have been met.

HACCP Hazard Analysis Critical Control Points – a technique by which hazards are identified and critical control points defined to ensure that the hazard does not occur.

ISO International Standards Organization.

Internal quality audit/schedule The audit of a quality management system by a team of trained internal auditors to a laid-down schedule.

Lead assessor An individual who has successfully completed a course to carry out assessment of quality management systems.

Management Representative The member of the management team nominated by the Chief Executive for the development of a quality management system for certification, and to manage the programme after certification has been achieved.

Management review Meeting held to review the key issues and performance of the quality management system.

Manuals Documents that define the required procedures and records; they can be at company, division, department or section level.

Nonconformance A variation from procedure, practice or performance standard.

Procedure Documents that define working practice, and generally relate to a specific task.

Product quality standard Document that defines the required quality attributes of a specified product. It can be supported by standard samples, pictures, etc.

Quality assurance All those planned and systematic actions necessary to provide adequate confidence that a structure, system, component or product will perform satisfactorily in service or use.

Quality circles Groups of people, generally drawn from a common work group, who meet to identify problems, and to generate and implement solutions using a structured approach.

Quality costs The costs of appraisal, prevention and failure.

Quality improvement teams Groups of people nominated by management to tackle defined problems.

Quality management systems The overall plan and arrangements by which quality matters are managed.

Quality record Retained information about key quality parameters identified in the quality plan.

Supplier management The activities of supplier approval, appraisal and review.

Surveillance visit The routine visit by assessors after certification to the standard has been awarded.

Total quality management An approach that encourages individual responsibility and continuous improvement to improve business efficiency and attitude.

Waste management Procedures by which waste, work in progress and nonconforming items are managed.

References

BSI (1994) *BS EN ISO 9001 Quality Systems – Model for Quality Assurance in Design, Development, Production, Installation and Servicing*, British Standards Institution, London.

Doeg, C. (1995) *Crisis Management in the Food and Drinks Industry: A Practical Approach*, Chapman & Hall, London.

EEC (1989) Council Directive of 14th June 1989 on the Official Control of Foodstuffs (89/397/EEC), EEC, Brussels.

European Foundation for Quality Management (1994) *Guidelines for Identifying and Addressing Business Excellence Issues – Self Assessment based on The European Model for Total Quality Management*, The European Foundation for Quality Management, Avenue Pleiades 19, 1200 Brussels, Belgium.

Groocock, J.M. (1974) *The Cost of Quality*, Pitman.

HMSO (1974) Health and Safety at Work Act 1974, HMSO, London.

HMSO (1988) Control of Substances Hazardous to Health (COSHH) Regulations, HMSO, London.

HMSO (1990) Food Safety Act, HMSO, London.

HMSO (1992) Management of Health and Safety at Work Regulations, HMSO, London.

Hubbard, M.R. (1990) *Statistical Quality Control for the Food Industry*, Van Nostrand Reinhold, New York.

Institute of Food Science and Technology (1991) *Food and Drink – Good Manufacturing Practice: A Guide to its Responsible Management*, 3rd edn, IFST, London.

Mortimore, S. and Wallace, C. (1994) *HACCP: A Practical Approach*, Chapman & Hall, London.

Oakland, J.S. (1986) *Statistical Process Control – A Practical Guide*, Butterworth-Heinemann, Oxford.

Oakland, J.S. (1989) *Total Quality Management*, Butterworth-Heinemann, Oxford.

Wilson, S. and Weir, G. (1995) *Food and Drink Laboratory Accreditation: A Practical Approach*, Chapman & Hall, London.

Other food-related documents

Code of Practice for Traders on Price Indications, HMSO, London.

Department of Health: Guidelines on the Food Hygiene (Amendment) Regulations 1990, HMSO, London.

Department of Health: Guidelines on the Food Hygiene Amendment Regulations – Guidelines for the Catering Industry, HMSO, London.

Food Safety Act 1990: Guidelines on the Statutory Defence of Due Diligence (1991), Published jointly by NCC, LACOTS, IEHO, NFU, The Retail Consortium and the FDF, London.

Index